**Michael Waeber / Hans**

# Valais West

**Translated by Gill Round**

50 selected day walks round Sion, Sierre, Martigny
and in the Val de Zinal, Val d'Hérens, Val de Bagnes
and Val d'Entremont

With 62 colour photos, 48 small maps to a scale of 1:50,000,
two small maps to a scale of 1:75,000, and
two contextualising maps to a scale of 1:450,000 and1:700,000

**ROTHER · MUNICH**

Frontispiece:
Pigne d'Arolla with the highest houses of Arolla.
Photo opposite title page (page 2):
The attractive vines are characteristic of western Valais.
Photos: Michael Waeber

Photo acknowledgements (page numbers):
Christoph Bauer (101, 106, 120), Walter Hellberg (73, 124),
Herbert Kunstmann (51).
All other photos are by the authors.

Cartography:
W. Mayr, Innsbruck; Ingenieurbüro Heidi Schmalfuß, Munich




1st edition 2002

ISBN 3-7633-4820-4

# Valais West

# Foreword

The Valais – high mountains, land of the four-thousanders, ice and snow at all times of the year, a dream for mountaineers, high mountain tourists and skiers. But hiking? Yes, there are many opportunities for hiking along ancient paths from the valleys up to the alpine pastures or to the lower summits and there are still many waiting to be discovered. These small mountains, most of them totally unknown, are incomparably beautiful viewpoints for the more famous snow-covered peaks opposite. There is an inexhaustible diversity of old paths from alp to alp, following water channels, across sunny slopes, through thin larch woods, and over meadows carpeted with flowers.

The long hiking season lasts from the middle of March to the middle of November, and you can experience the change in the seasons at various levels of altitude: from the Mediterranean floor of the Rhône valley right up to the edge of the glaciers. The region has little rainfall and abounds in days of sunshine. High mountain chains, to the north and south, ward off incessant bad-weather fronts that have forced the inhabitants for centuries to devise costly irrigation systems.

Hiking in the Valais canton is described in one hundred walks in two guides: 'Valais East' and 'Valais West'. Here, in the 'Valais West' guide, you will find 50 walks in the French speaking part of the canton. We have kept to the official language boundary between Swiss German / Swiss French along the Raspille (a stream between Salgesch and Siders). The 50 walks on the flanks of the Rhône valley and in its side valleys promise impressive views of the natural and agricultural landscape of the Valais. All the walks run along either footpaths, marked mountain paths or obvious paths. No special gear or training is necessary, but you should have had some experience in walking along narrow and sometimes exposed paths. Many of the suggestions for walks are also suitable for families with children (these have been specially signed out). Due to the snow in high places, however, other walks might still be impassable in early summer.

For this new edition we would like to thank a circle of helpers for their various tips and improvements, especially the Valrando assosiation for mountainpaths in Vallis, and also the individual tourist offices, in particular the central 'Valais tourism' in Sitten which gave us all kinds of assistance.

We wish all friends of nature and mountains who take our guide with them on hikes along the Valais paths, carefree days full of sunshine and adventure.

Rottau and Hittenkirchen, spring 2002
Michael Waeber, Hans Steinbichler

## Contents

**Abbreviations:**

MO Martigny-Orsières Railway
MC Martigny-Châtelard Railway
PTT Swiss Post (post, telegraph, telephone)
SAC Swiss Alpine Club
SBB Swiss National Railway
WW Signpost

# Tourist tips

## Using the guide

The suggestions for walks are generally arranged from east to west, ie. westwards from the language boundary at the Raspille. Walks in the side valleys are to be found listed under the name of the appropriate major valley, the only exceptions being where some paths, adjacent to each other, need to be more conveniently described in the same section. Tourist and cultural information about the locations are contained in the following chapter. In the 'bad-weather chapter' you will find a collection of alternative activities for 'rainy days and rest days'.
Each walk begins with the most important information presented in a fact file and includes access by public transport to the starting point. After a short characterisation of the walk there's a description of the route. The colour map provides a good overview of the walk and there's a colour photo giving you an impression of the region. In the index at the back you will find all the mountains, base points and objectives for every stage of the walk. The contextualising map on 32/33 helps you to locate the walks easily.

## Grade

All the walks described in the guide are easy and can be undertaken with suitable mountain gear (hiking boots and appropriate clothing) often into late autumn. However, there are still times when you need to be sure-footed and must not be prone to vertigo. In order to assess the grade more accurately the walks are colour-coded as follows:

### BLUE

The paths are good and marked throughout, comfortably wide and only moderately steep. Even in less good weather they can be undertaken with relative safety. Children and older people, too, can go on these walks without any great difficulty.

### RED

These mountain paths are sufficiently well marked, but predominantly narrow and in a few places rather exposed. On some short sections there might also be cables for safety reasons. These walks should therefore only be undertaken by sure-footed mountain walkers with the appropriate gear.

*The road at Euseigne goes through an area of imposing earth pyramids in Val d'Hérens. Relics of enormous scree moraines on the Ice Age glacier.*

SAURER

**BLACK**
These mountain paths are also sufficiently well marked, but mostly narrow and with some lengthy steep sections. They can be very exposed in places and sometimes you will need to use your hands. These walks should only be undertaken by absolutely sure-footed and fit hikers with alpine experience.

**Dangers**
Almost all the walks follow well-marked paths. Reference is made in the text to places that are particularly exposed or demanding. Some routes go over the 3000m mark and you have to be prepared for snow, even in summer. If you are doubtful about the conditions, it is best to make enquiries in the valley (eg. in the tourist and mountain guide offices) or walk round the area first on lower paths.

**Equipment**
The most important piece of equipment is a good pair of sturdy boots with sticky soles – so-called trekking boots have proved to be very successful. Long comfortable trousers, warm and protective clothing, hat and gloves for high altitude routes in summer as well, (even when it's hot in high summer in the valley). On some walks you might reach an altitude of more than 3000m. For autumn, when the days are getting shorter, it is recommended that you carry a head-torch.
You should, of course, take plenty enough to drink with you (but not in environmentally unfriendly cans – take your own water bottles) and also enough to eat.

**Maps**
Many of the walks can be undertaken by using the sections of map in this book. However it is recommended that you equip yourself with the excellent Swiss topographical maps (a map of the whole of Switzerland or special regional ones put together by the tourist associations). These elaborate works of art, with their clarity and detail, are the most useful for countless other projects. The prices are about 13 SFr for the normal maps and the individual maps with walks and concise route descriptions are priced according to size, from 10 to 25 SFr. They are available from bookshops, kiosks, railway stations and tourist offices.

**Walking times**
Giving details about time can be problematic. In this guide you are given the average length of time you would normally expect to take for each walk without having done any great 'training', and this does not include breaks and photo stops. The times are simply an aid to planning. If, in good condi-

tions, you stay out longer, then presumably you are getting more out of these walks.
Basically, your schedule should be determined by the weather, the times of buses and trains, or approaching nightfall, and not by your enthusiasm for setting new walking records.

**Food and accommodation**
In this section you will find the restaurants and huts which are open in summer along the routes. Overnight stops are mentioned where available. For safety reasons in early summer or autumn you should enquire in the valley about the facilities.
The restaurants or kiosks at the mountain railway stations are usually open when there are trains running.

**Aiding your ascent**
Cable-cars, lifts and taxi busses have been included in the route description where applicable. Some services only operate in summer (all train and bus routes are contained in the 'Valais timetable', available in tourist offices and at train and bus ticket offices) and if they are not in operation in autumn the walks might be longer, but they are quieter too!

**Getting there**
For visitors from England the Valais is relatively far away so weekend trips are out of the question. Most holiday makers travel in their own car although that can be a problem here too (traffic jams just like in the cities, bad air and very few parking spaces).
However the Valais can be reached easily by rail and there are high speed trains from England via France or Belgium. For those approaching via Germany there are some magical journeys, for example, with the Furka-Oberalp railway from Chur to Brig or the Lötschberg line – the journey is then already part of your holiday.
Anyway, as practically all the walks described here are accessible by bus or train, you should seriously consider whether a car free holiday is a possibility. The admittedly high prices for single tickets become more reasonable when you take advantage of the numerous special deals on offer from the railway companies. When comparing the price with driving your own car you should not forget to take into account the hefty parking fees as well as the motorway tax disc and possible tolls and luggage transfer costs. Not to mention the extremely tiring journey in heavy traffic – not everyone is ready to go on a big walk the next day and precious holiday time is perhaps wasted. And what's more, most visitors pay much higher prices for ski passes without question in winter, but in summer they tend to reject public transport for the sake of just a few 'Fränkli'.

**Protecting the environment.**
We should stress at this point the need for care in conserving nature. This wonderful landscape, in parts still the same as it was thousands of years ago, but also shaped by many centuries of human use, is, after all, what the holiday-maker is looking for and wants to find in the future. Especially on holiday one ought to be able to do without anything which results in pollution of the environment, excessive use of energy, as well as the disruption of cultivation and inhabitants.
You should therefore leave all places as you would wish to find them, by using the least amount of packaging (walkers should take back to the valley all litter and dispose of it there) and of course by limiting the production of air pollution with a sparing use of the car. Of all holiday activities, walking offers the most intimate contact with nature, but is ideal, even in the age of mass tourism, for showing people what is worth protecting in the most environmentally friendly way.
Unfortunately the degradation of the landscape which walkers find in all parts of the Alps has to be confronted in the Valais as well. In particular we should mention downhill skiing for which whole valley communities have been sacrificed by the cabling and excavation of vast areas. Villages and mountain settlements, once having evolved harmoniously, have now been transformed into city-like hotel and apartment complexes. Also twenty storey high-rise buildings have made their way into the alpine meadows in the Valais.
But the worse thing is that there still seems to be no end to the development in sight. The running sores of ski-lifts are eating their way further and further into the remotest valleys and if the landscape and the climate do not suit, bulldozers and snow-blasters lend a helping hand and make anything possible.
When there's snow on the ground the winter visitor experiences an apparently intact world, but then the wounds become obvious by summer at the latest. Of course, at present, big money is still being spent in winter and for many places this is seemingly the only possible means of survival, but for how much longer can we afford this type of holiday with its exhaustive use of energy and the landscape?
Happily some of the problems created by earlier attitudes towards alpine holidays are no longer being ignored. People do not escape from the hostile environment of the city only to rediscover it in a holiday resort. Already some places have begun to correct former mistakes by making an enormous capital investment to rebuild roads and traditional resting places. Perhaps the mountain walker can provide an example to skiing tourism less harmful to nature, and encourage a middle way between the total impoverishment of valley communities which have been dependent on tourism and a 'techno-world' à la Val d'Isère.

*The Combin dominates Val de Bagnes. Verbier lies above the valley (Walk 32).*

Also the tourist business is complying with the principles of supply and demand. Downhill skiing is as popular as ever and correspondingly the supply is well developed. Those responsible for tourism must be aware of the fact that the demands of the winter sportsman on a region are difficult to reconcile with the wishes of other visitors throughout the year.
Every single person can remind their host of the demand for an unspoilt landscape – by conversation, expressing your preferences in the tourist office and lively discussion of environmental problems. Perhaps then you will have made a contribution to the decision by the inhabitants in future projects, to place more importance on nature again (ultimately their own basis for life) and less on making a fast buck. The Binn valley is a happy example of this.

# Locations

In practically every place in the Valais you have a large choice of accommodation of all categories, whether it be hotels, b&b or holiday flats, all too numerous to mention. Prices are comparable with those in other parts of the Alps. It is of course advisable to book early in high summer as it is everywhere else. However in early summer and autumn there are sufficient vacancies. Campsites and group accommodation are pointed out as they are not available everywhere.
The listing of tourist facilities cannot, of course, lay claim to being complete, nor can all villages be named for reasons of space – individual tourist offices will gladly be able to give further information. The height locations given of smaller places relate to the central point (church, station, main crossroads), but with settlements which are spread out, particularly those on hillsides, the height of the general area is given.

**Sierre (Siders), 540m**
Beautiful little town in the central Valais near to the language boundary, opposite the mouth of the Val d'Anniviers into the Rhône valley; IC railway station of the SBB line.
Several historic buildings, castle-like secular buildings like the residential tower of the Château des Vidomnes (castle of the viceroy) characterise the town. Beautiful old suburbs like 'Villa' or 'Muraz'; museum of weapons and Rilke room in Villa.
The climate is sunny and dry and lends the region a Mediterranean appeal with bustling activity in the narrow streets, street cafés, wine bars and many good restaurants. Many sports facilities like tennis, indoor and lake swimming pool, horse-riding or golf. The surrounding area is characterised by fruit orchards and vineyards as far as the eye can see, although high up on the south slope of the Bernese Alps can be seen the less pleasant effects of winter tourism in the form of the high-rise hotel of Crans-Montana. There's a good selection of excursions on offer in the area around Sierre, as for example Val d'Anniviers, Leukerbad, the underground lake in St. Léonard, the Pfyn forest and the wild Illgraben. Babyland-Park has many attractions. Group accommodation, campsite. Office du tourisme 3960 Sierre, tel: 027/4558535.

**Chandolin, 1920m**
Situated to the east on a sunny terrace above the Zinal valley, former alpine settlement below the Illhorn. Walking country with magnificent views (eg. Gorwetsch ridge and Illsee which has unfortunately been massively developed in the area around the ski slopes. Chair lift to Chandolin alp. Group accommodation. Office du tourisme, 3961 Chandolin, tel: 027/4751838.

*At the Bisse du Lens; view into the Rhône valley towards Sierre (Walk 14).*

**St. Luc, 1655m**
Funicular railway to Tignousa alp, from there many possibilities for hiking, eg. to the Bella Tola, one of the best known views of a three-thousander, or along the planetary path to Zinal. Unfortunately increasing intrusions into nature by ski slopes and alpine paths almost as far as Bella Tola. Old mill. Tennis, fishing, camping, group accommodation. Office du tourisme 3961 St. Luc, tel: 027/4751412.

**Vissoie, 1204m**
Main town of Val d'Anniviers before it divides to Zinal and Moiry. Beautiful old village centre with historic buildings: tower dating from the 13th/14th century, St Mary's chapel from 1688, church from 1809 with bell tower from 1745. Convenient and centrally placed base for all activities in this valley. Museum of local history and culture, heated swimming pool, campsite. Office du tourisme 3961 Vissoie, tel: 027/4751412.

**St. Jean, 1327m – Mission, 1300m – Ayer, 1476m**
St. Jean is situated to the west of the Navisence on the road to Grimentz. Mission and Ayer are opposite on the road to Zinal. Beautiful view of the end of the Zinal valley with the Zinalrothorn. Old houses. In Ayer there are still old ladders made from one tree trunk. Tennis, climbing wall. Group accommodation, camping (Mission).

**Zinal, 1675m**
Former summer alp village, not inhabited all year. Not linked by road until the end of the 50s, before that seen by tourists as a blank on the map in the middle of extremely wild landscape. Museum of local history and culture (old farm house). Together with a short summer season there's also now a lively tourist trade in winter which is due to the cable car development of the Sorebois region, although it's not comparable with mass tourism in the neighbouring Matter valley. Starting point for many great hikes in every direction. Group accomodation, campsite; tennis, indoor swimming pool, minigolf, wild water rafting, guided hikes and alpine tours (mountain guide office). Office du tourisme, 3961 Zinal, tel: 027/4751370.

**Grimentz, 1564m**
Situated at the start of the Moiry valley a little way above the turn-off from the Zinal valley. Popular beautiful village to walk to with its wooden sun-baked houses adorned with flowers. The centre of the village is fortunately closed to vehicles. Cable railway to Bendolla alp, the broad hollows between Roc d'Orzival and Becs de Bosson have been developed as a lift region – hopefully this will be enough to satisfy them. Tennis, indoor swimming pool, group accommodation, campsite. Office du tourisme 3961 Grimentz, tel: 027/4751493.

**Vercorin, 1322m**
Situated in a sheltered small hollow high above the mouth of Val d'Anniviers into the Rhône valley, accessible by road and cable car from Chalais. Cable car to the Crêt du Midi. Nature trails with informative brochures near to Vercorin. The nearby Val de Réchy is a nature reserve. Good choice of walks. Tennis, minigolf, horse-riding. Group accommodation. Office du tourisme, 3967 Vercorin, tel: 027/4555855.

**Veyras, 647m – Miège, 702m – Venthône, 799m – Molléns, 1075m**
'Wine-growing villages' above Sierre with some very pretty village centres. Much quieter and more attractive than in Crans-Montana situated above. Gothic church (1667) and castle (mentioned in 1268) in Venthône, as well as other historic buildings in the other villages. Office du Tourisme d'Aminona, tel: 027/4810101.

**Crans-Montana - Vermala, 1200 - 1700m**
Settlement spread out on a large terrace above Sierre on the southern slope of the Bernese Alps (Wildstrubel massif); unfortunately there has been some urban development here, partly in the ugly, uniform style of French or Italian ski resorts, which does nothing to enhance it. A very elegant sports area has been created here: golf, tennis, squash, ice skating rink and horse-riding arena, minigolf, swimming pools, climbing wall, congress hall. The area around Bella Lui and Mont Bonvin has been largely developed for skiing. Nevertheless the surrounding area provides many opportunities for walking, especially along the historic water channels. There are cable cars and cable railways in summer to the Bella Lui, Plaine Morte and Petit Bonvin, a lift from Sierre to Montana and a free bus service near to the towns. Group accommodation, campsite. Office du tourisme, 3963 Crans and 3962 Montana: tel: 027/4850404 and 027/4850800.

**Chermignon, 910 - 1150m - Flanthey, 750m**
**Lens, 1128m - Icogne, 1026m**
Chermignon, Lens and Icogne are situated on a small platform south-west below Crans-Montana with agricultural surroundings; Flanthey, together with the villages of Chelin and Ollon, is in the vineyard area above the Rhône valley. Beautiful towns with extensive views. Linked to St. Leonard and Sierre by a dense network of roads, as well as to Crans-Montana and over the Liène gorge to Ayent. Office du tourisme, 1978 Lens, tel: 027/4831081.

**Grimisuat, 881m - Arbaz, 1146m**
**Ayent, 840 - 1050m - Anzère, 1650m**
Villages stretching from the vineyard area up into the pasture area on the slope facing south-east above the Liène gorge which comes down from the Rawil pass. Anzère is a former alpine settlement, now a modern sports resort (cable railway to the Pas de Maimbre), open air and indoor swimming pool, tennis, minigolf. Ayent consists of several villages. St. Romain has a parish church dating from 1862 and other historic buildings. Office du tourisme, 1974 Arbaz, tel: 027/3983677; 1972 Anzère, tel: 027/3992803.

**Savièse, 650 - 1340m**
Community made up of several villages on the south slopes directly above Sion, vines in the lower regions, cultivation of grain and cattle breeding further above, also where commuters to Sion live. Various historic buildings, eg. the churches in St. Germain (1523) or Drône (St.-Christoph chapel, 1694). The Bisse from Savièse dates from historic times when, with its daring construction, it took the water from the Morge gorge through the chaos of rocks west of the Prabé onto the plateau. There's a tunnel today and you can no longer walk along the Bisse.

**Chalais, 521m - Réchy, 524m - Granges, 503m - Grône, 513m**
Situated in the Rhône valley between Sierre and St. Léonard on the fertile 'shady side'. Intensive agriculture (vines, fruit, vegetables), also settlement of small businesses. Campsite in Granges, group accommodation.

**St. Léonard, 498m - Uvrier, 497m**
Situated at the mouth of the Liène which comes down from the Rawil pass, intensive agriculture (fruit and wine growing), as well as limestone and gypsum quarrying. A special attraction is the 'lac souterrain', the largest underground lake in Europe, with guided boat trips. Swimming pool. Camping.

**Sion (Sitten), 500m**
Capital of the Valais canton and since 580 a cathedral town, situated in a very sunny dry climate. Surrounded by vineyards and fruit orchards, as well as some industry, airport and IC connection.
There are two noticeable hills in the town: on one of them stands the famous pilgrimage church of Notre Dame (Valère) which is well-worth visiting and the museum of cultural history, on the other (Tourbillon) you will unfortunately only find the ruins of a castle dating from the 13th century.
Other sights: town hall from 1657/65, Notre Dame cathedral (12th century and late gothic), witches' tower on the former city wall, Theodul church (1514/16). Centre for excursions throughout the whole of western Valais. Group accommodation, campsites. Office du tourisme, 1950 Sion, tel: 027/3228586.

**Conthey, 511m - Vétroz, 487m - Ardon, 490m**
Situated in the bottom of the Rhône valley near Sion, extensive winegrowing region at the foot of the Bernese Alps. From Conthey the road leads to the Sanetsch pass and to Derborence via Sensine, Daillon, Erde, Premploz and Aven. Excursions can be made into the neighbouring countryside. Campsite in Vétroz. Office du tourisme, 1964 Mayens de Conthey, tel: 027/3467232.

**Bramois, 511m**
Town created by fruit and vine cultivation at the mouth of the Val d'Hérens into the Rhône valley. A bit further in the gorge below some rocks is the Longeborgne hermitage, founded in 1522. The stone bridge over the Borgne dates from 1550. Ancient wooden and stone houses.

**Nax, 1265m - Vernamiège, 1301m - Mase, 1345m**
**Suen, 1429m - St. Martin, 1411m - Eison, 1650m**
Small villages on the sun terraces above Val d'Hérens; they cling onto the steep slopes like a string of pearls. Interesting village centres, tennis, alpine

*Autumn on the Lac de Derberance – the wood in the background hiding the enormous firs mentioned in Walk 26.*

guided tours, Combioula thermal spring.
The hiking area stretches above the villages and in the doline landscape round Nax you find many rare plants and species of birds. Lift from Nax towards Mont Noble. Group accommodation. Bus connection to Sion. Office du tourisme, 1961 Nax, tel: 027/2031738; 1969 St. Martin, tel: 027/2812474.

**Vex, 939m – Les Agettes, 1173m – Les Collons, 1795m**
**Hérémence, 1237m – Mâche, 1310m**

These villages are situated high above Val d'Hérens on the left hand side of the valley; Vex lies on the main road into the valley. Church from the 11th century. Turn-off into Val des Dix and to the former alpine settlements 'Mayens de Sion', Les Agettes and Les Collons which are today ski resorts in the area of 'Quatre vallées' with tennis, indoor pools and horse-riding. Campsite in Vex. Office du tourisme, 1988 Les Collons-Thyon, tel: 027/2812727; 1992 Les Agettes, tel: 027/2073350; 1987 Hérémence, tel: 027/2811533.

**Euseigne, 975m – La Luette, 997m – Praz-Jean, 1051m**
Small villages on the main road into Val d'Hérens, junction of the narrow road from Euseigne into Val d'Hérémence to Mâche and from Praz-Jean to the villages high above the valley round St. Martin – Suen – Mase. The earth pyramids at Euseigne are one attraction. The stone bridge over the Borgne at Praz-Jean dates from 1636.

**Evolène, 1371m**
Main village of Val d'Hérens with lots of houses still preserved in their original style. Characteristic are the narrow, wooden houses of several storeys built out of dark larch wood, but also the stone painted façades. Val d'Hérens still provides a pleasantly quiet holiday area in summer amidst magnificent scenery. If the Dent Blanche is the only four-thousander standing at the valley head, the other peaks are no less impressive. Lift from Lana (Lannaz) to the Meina Alps (Chemeuille). Group acconmodation, campsite. Office du tourisme, 1983 Evolène, tel: 027/2831235.

**Les Haudères, 1436m**
Situated in pleasant walking country at the junction of Val d'Hérens (Arolla and Ferpécle) without the great hustle and bustle of tourism. There's a variety of walks on offer from short ones to big mountain routes, an ideal holiday area for anyone wanting to keep away from the more popular routes in none-the-less beautiful scenery. Well-preserved village centre together with new buildings. Exhibition of geology and glaciology. Tennis. Campsite. Office du tourisme, 1984 Les Haudères, tel: 027/2831015.

**La Sage, 1667m – Villa, 1742m – La Forclaz, 1744m**
Small settlements preserved extensively in their original style in the upper Val d'Hérens and in the Ferpècle side valley. Interesting walking country, eg. towards Col de Torrent and Bricola alp. Group accommodation. Société de développement, 1985 La Sage, tel: 027/2831280.

**Arolla, 1998m**
Uppermost settlement in the side valley of Val d'Hérens with the same name. Not all that long ago this fabulous valley head had been accessible in winter only on foot. Now some modest tourism has been developed and the road has been extended. In winter a lift as far as Pas de Chèvres, in summer

a walker's paradise and base for tours into the high mountains, hardly a stone's throw away from the large ice flows. The houses (hotels and apartments) lie scattered in the thin woods of Swiss stone pine and larch. Water power is used here as it is pretty well all over the Valais. Hopefully this valley head will remain protected from further ski development and the tourist facilities up to now will suffice. Group accommodation, campsite. Office du tourisme, 1986 Arolla, tel: 027/2831083.

**Veysonnaz, 1233m, Nendaz, 950 – 1600m**
The villages lie on both sides at the start of Val de Nendaz. Interesting old village centres in Basse Nendaz and Veysonnaz, but the chalets and hotels are closed in summer and only booked out in winter. But if you look carefully, it's not difficult to find beautiful walking country. Summer skiing area at Mont Fort. Group accommodation. Office du tourisme, 1993 Veysonnaz, tel: 027/2071053; 1997 Nendaz, tel: 027/2895589.

**Isérables, 1106m**
Interesting settlement above the Fare valley with many old houses; cable car from Riddes in the Rhône valley. Narrow village centre, the land was more important for agricultural use – so it is easy to understand why there is only limited parking space for visitors' cars. At the forest boundary on the Balavaux alps there are some beautiful larch trees worth taking a look at, some of them over 1000 years old with gigantic broad trunks. Group accommodation.

**Mayens de Riddes, 1520m**
Former summer alp, the few huts were previously only inhabited during the driving of cattle to the alpine pastures in May / June and then in October/ November. Today a modern winter sports resort in the region of the 'Quatre vallées'; in spite of its wonderful location, it's like almost all modern ski places in summer: over-sized apartment blocks with the shutters rolled down and constant building activity. However the region has some marvellous walking country. Group accommodation. Office du tourisme, 1918 Mayens de Riddes, tel: 027/3061851.

**Ovronnaz, 1200 – 1420m**
Holiday resort situated on the sunny slope above vineyards and fruit orchards. PTT bus service to Sion via Leytron (almost hourly service with a good hour's journey from Sion, 28km). Tennis, thermal bath, ski area, guided hikes (also with information on topical themes: cheese production, botany etc.). Group accommodation, campsite, fishing. The beautiful Tour du Muveran crosses the municipal district (Rambert hut). Office du tourisme, 1911 Ovronnaz, tel: 027/3064293.

**Chamoson, 610 – 750m – Leytron, 501m – Saillon, 510m**
These villages lie in the Rhône valley wine region above Ovronnaz, at the foot of the strange Ardevaz wedge of rock. The style of buildings displays a strong Mediterranean character. The small villages of Produit, Montagnon

*View of the Mont Blanc massif from Pierre Avoi (Walk 32).*

and Dugny are situated on a cone of debris which is slowly moving up the valley and keeps causing damage to roads and buildings.
Thermal bath centre 'Bains de Saillon' with lots of sports facilities. Group accommodation. Office du tourisme, 1955 Chamoson, tel: 027/3065533; 1913 Saillon, tel: 027/7431111.

**Riddes, 475m – Saxon, 533m – Charrat, 461m**
Situated on the orographical left, therefore south side of the lower Rhône valley, with intensive agriculture, especially fruit growing, also wine growing on the lower slopes. Church in Riddes from the 17th century, stopping places for the SBB line Martigny – Sion. Good roads to the former alpine settlements (Mayens). In contrast to the sun-baked southern slopes on the Bernese Alps side, these 'shady' slopes offer fertile soil with no shortage of water. Beautiful mountain paths. The Suone running into the Nendaz valley is 33 kilometres long. Cable car from Riddes to Isérables. Interesting flora (yellow Pheasant's Eye in spring). Group accommodation, campsite in Saxon.

**Fully, 473m**
Scattered wine and fruit growing community at the south-west foot of the Bernese Alps, only 5km away from Martigny and starting point for excursions to the 'Follatères', a very interesting dry biotope at the climatically extreme corner of the sharp bend of the Rhône. Group accommodation.

**Martigny (Martito), 476m**
Pretty little town with Mediterranean charm at the sharp bend of the Rhône, junction of the roads to Chamonix and Aosta. SBB stop, also trains to Chamonix (MC railway) and Orsières / Le Châble (MO railway; Val d'Entremont, towards Grand St. Bernard and Val de Bagnes). Inhabited in the period BC: amphitheatre, interesting archaeological excavations (archaeological museum, Gallo-Roman museum with art exhibition). Historic buildings, eg. the medieval castle of La Bâtiaz with a Savoyard tower high above the town. Beautiful avenue of plane trees with shady street cafés. Group accommodation, campsite. Starting point for marvellous walks, big round walks start from here like the 'Tour du Combins, Muveran, Trient, Dents du Midi' or the better-known 'Tour du Mont Blanc'. Beautiful pasture and wooded country on the ridge to the Pas du Lin and Mont Arpille. Office régional du tourisme, 1920 Martigny, tel: 027/7212220.

**Les Valettes, 626m – Bovernier, 615m – Sembrancher, 717m**
The places lie on the road to Grand St. Bernard, the Val de Bagnes turns off in Sembrancher. MO railway from Martigny, continues to Orsières or Le Châble. Beautiful Mediterranean-type village in Sembrancher with baroque church from 1686. The good transport links make them convenient bases

for walking in this region, also an excursion to Aosta is easily possible. In Les Valettes a small road turns off to Champex. The stream of this side valley cuts through the Durnand gorge which is worth a visit. Campsite in Sembrancher.

**Vollèges, 843m – Vens, 1111m – Levron, 1307m**

Vollèges with interesting gothic tower from 1507 lies on an overgrown cone of debris below the western cliffs of Pierre Avoi. A road network links the village with Sembrancher and the sun-baked settlements on the mountain ridge round Pas du Lin, Col du Tronc and Col des Planches.

The village of Levron is of historic interest since an extremely long water channel not only crossed the wild rock basin below Pierre Avoi, but also had to negotiate the wide Verbier crater to reach Mont Fort (Bisse du Levron, built in the 14th century).

**Le Châble, 821m – Bruson, 1042m**

Settlements in the lower Val de Bagnes, road and cable car to Verbier from Le Châble (terminus of the rail line from Martigny).

From Bruson a small road goes to La Côt, previously an alpine pasture, today a scattered holiday village in a location with beautiful views. Chair lift from Bruson. Lift area in winter (with horrifying plans for expansion). Art exhibitions in Le Châble. Office du tourisme, 1934 Le Châble, tel: 027/7761682.

**Verbier, 1500m**

One of the best-known winter sport resorts in the area of the 'Quatre vallées' – between Pierre Avoi and Mont Fort practically every slope has been made accessible by lifts. At Mont Fort there is also summer skiing. With the exception of these tracks, the region provides wonderful walking holidays with stunning views.

In the village you will find almost every facility that a 'modern' holidaymaker could wish for. Group accommodation. Paradise for paragliding and hang gliding, as well as mountain biking. Office du tourisme, 1936 Verbier, tel: 027/7716222.

**Prarreyer, 854m – Versegères, 896m – Champsec, 901m**
**Sarreyer, 1239m – Lourtier, 1072m – Fionnay, 1490m**

Small villages in the Val de Bagnes as it gets narrower and wilder, only Sarreyer (restored water mill from 1837) lies above the valley floor. The Grande Dixence power station is conspicuous with two smaller support reservoirs and the transformer station (cavern power station) in Fionnay. The valley widens out again further up with the settlement of Bonatchièse, and then the road winds up to the head of the dam of Lac de Mauvoisin (250m high convex dam, the most impressive building work of this type in Switzerland); post bus service in summer. A small road turns off above Lourtier to the Cabane Brunet near the north face of the Petit Combin. Group accommodation. Office du Tourisme, 1948 Sarreyer, tel: 027/7781728.

**Orsières, 901m**
Main town of Val d'Entremont at the turn-off into Val Ferret, interesting town centre. Terminus of the train line from Martigny, continue by 'Bernard-Express' to Aosta. Roads into Val Ferret and to Champex le Lac. Horse-riding, minigolf, indoor swimming pool. Starting point for many activities. Group accommodation. Office du tourisme, 1937 Orsières, tel: 027/7831531.

**Liddes, 1346m – Chandonne, 1454m – Vichères, 1423m**
Small villages on and above the Grand St. Bernard road at the mouth of the Combe de l'A, a remote high valley. Peaceful walking country, just a very small lift area near Vichères. Office du Tourisme de la Vallée du Grand St. Bernard, 1945 Liddes, tel: 027/7833879.

**Bourg St. Pierre, 1632m**
Uppermost village before the Grand St. Bernard, old village centre, the main road goes past the village above. Alpine garden with rare plants. On the west side of the Grand Combin there's an extensive area for hiking and excursions. Interesting stone bridge (built in about 800) across the gorge of the Valsorey stream and traces of a Roman road. Indoor pool. The hospice with museum is situated on the Grand St. Bernard. St. Bernard breeding farm. Société de développement, 1946 Bourg St. Pierre, tel: 027/7871200.

**Champex le Lac, 1466m**
A holiday resort at the pretty lake of Lac de Champex, situated on a col between the foothills of the mountains around the Trient glacier, part of the Mont Blanc area, and the totally isolated Catogne. Botanical garden. Chair lift to La Breya, for mountaineers an approach of the Trient glacier region. Tennis, heated open air pool. Campsite. Office du tourisme, 1938 Champex, tel: 027/7831227.

**Som la Proz, 968m – Issert, 1055m – Praz de Fort, 1151m**
**La Fouly, 1593m – Ferret, 1700m**
These villages in Val Ferret at the point where Mont Blanc and the Valais meet offer holidays in splendid surroundings without too much hustle and bustle. Stopping places for the big Mont Blanc round walk. Bus service to Orsières. Small lift area in La Fouly. Water mill dating from 1633 in Issert.

Museum of local history and culture in Praz-de-Fort. Campsite in La Fouly, group accommodation. Office du tourisme, 1944 La Fouly, tel: 027/ 7832717.

**Salvan, 934m – Les Granges, 1059m**
**Les Marécottes, 1100m – Le Trétien, 1021m**

Holiday villages situated on a platform above the lower, wild Trient gorge on the railway line Martigny – Chamonix. Beautiful views and peaceful walking area, eg. the remote Vallon de Van (campsite). Cable car Les Marécottes – Le Creusaz. Swimming pools, tennis, minigolf. Alpine zoo in Les Marécottes. Group accommodation. Campsite in Les Marécottes. Office du tourisme, 1922 Salvan, tel: 027/7611589.

**Trient, 1279m – Finhaut, 1298m – Le Châtelard, 1127m**

Villages in marvellous hiking area Martigny – Chamonix (on the railway or post bus link between). Here too you will find many peaceful activities with wonderful views at the edge of the Valais. Lac d' Emosson, built between 1967 – 1975, with the steepest funicular railway in Europe and with a 180m high dam; above the reservoir can be found petrified dinosaur tracks on the rocks. Indoor swimming pool. Group accommodation, campsite on the Col de la Forclaz. Société de développement, 1929 Trient, tel: 027/7221929; Office du tourisme, 1925 Finhaut, tel: 027/7681278.

**Vernayaz, 452m – Miéville, 451m – Dorénaz, 451m**
**Collonges, 452m – Evionnaz, 469m**

These villages lie on both sides of the Rhône flowing here to the north in the direction of Lake Geneva. Agriculture, small businesses, quarries. There was previously much more quarrying activity and there are many traces of this in the mountains ('marble' from Dorénaz, mining of anthracite). The Trient gorge near Vernayaz is well worth a visit, right next to it the MC railway winds its way up the mountain along a breath-taking track towards Chamonix. Near Miéville the lovely Pissevache waterfall. From Dorénaz a small cable car and road to Allesse, a beautifully situated alpine and holiday settlement. Campsite. Office du tourisme 1902 Evionnaz, tel: 027/7671738.

**St. Maurice, 422m – Mex, 1118m**

Little town of historic importance: abbey with the tombstone of the martyr, Mauritius, from 515, valuable church treasures in the basilica. The geographical location at the narrow part of the Rhône valley also lead to military importance and there's a military museum in the castle.

*The breath-taking stretch towards Derborence (Walk 26).*

Stone bridge over the Rhône. The Grotte aux Fées is also worth visiting. A thousand metre long tunnel leads to an underground lake, and a 50m high waterfall cascades down into it. A narrow road leads from the Bois Noir situated in the south (pine wood on a former rubbish tip, conservation area) to Mex, high in the valley above a rock face. Close to St. Maurice lies Lavay les Bains, a thermal bath and from there a narrow road leads to Morcles. Campsite, group accommodation. Office du tourisme, 1890 St. Maurice, tel: 024/4852777.

**Monthey, 406m – Collombey, 392m – Vérossaz, 700 – 870m**
**Les Giettes, 850 – 1300m**

Monthey is a small industrial and garrison town beyond the narrow part of the Rhône, turn-off for Val d'Illiez with many opportunities for hiking on the Dents du Midi or the foothills to the north as far as Lake Geneva. Dense rail network: Aigle, Champéry, St. Gingolph, St. Maurice – Martigny. Narrow roads to the holiday settlements of Les Giettes (group accommodation) and Vérossaz. Office du tourisme, 1870 Monthey, tel: 024/4757963.

**Troistorrents, 765m – Val d'Illiez, 995m**
**Champéry, 1053m – Morgins, 1333m**

The communities of Val d'Illiez and the adjoining Val de Morgins offer a self-contained holiday region north of the Dents du Midi massif and the neighbouring Dents Blanches, part of 'Portes du Soleil' – crossing the border to France.
Rich selection of sporting activities: mountain-biking, tennis, squash, golf, indoor swimming pools; beautiful walking country, eg. Tour du Dents du Midi or Dents Blanches. Good transport connections with the AOMC railway (Aigle – Ollon – Monthey – Champéry). Group accommodation, campsites (Morgins, Champéry). Office du tourisme 'Portes du Soleil', 1874 Champéry, tel: 024/4792920; 1875 Morgins, tel: 024/4772361; 1873 Val d'Illiez, tel: 024/4772077.

**Muraz, 402m – Vionnaz, 392m – Vouvry, 380 – 440m**
**Torgon, 900 – 1100m – Miex, 900 – 1050m**

These villages lie in the lowest part of the Valais, in the Rhône valley between Monthey and Lake Geneva and on the slopes of the short side valleys above and to the west.
While intensive farming is pursued in the valley communities together with small businesses, tourist development in Miex is modest and in Torgnon, pronounced. The latter village isadjucent to the lift area 'Portes du Soleil'. Little known walking country on the border ridge to France. A scenic highpoint is the Lac de Tanay above Miex. Campsite in Le Bouveret. Office du tourisme, 1891 Torgon, tel: 024/4813131.

## Tips for rainy days and rest days

The following is a short overview of the most important attractions in the Valais. Without claiming to be complete, it will hopefully make the choice of activities which do not include a summit climb, that much easier.

**Thermal baths** in Mörel / Breiten, Brigerbad, Leukerbad, Saillon les Bains, Val d'Illiez and Lavey les Bains.
**Wild river rafting** in the Upper Goms.
**Underground lakes and caves** in St. Léonard (Lac Souterrain), Anzère (Rawil) and St. Maurice (Grotte aux Fées).Glacier ice caves on the Furka pass (Rhône glacier) and in Saas Fee (Fee glacier).
**Gorges** at Brig (Massa), on the Simplon pass (Gondo), at Susten / Agarn (Illgraben and Feschelklamm), in Val d'Anniviers (at Pontis), at Sion (Lizerne gorge) and at Martigny (Gorges du Dumand and Gorges du Trient).
**Waterfalls** at Rèchy and at Martigny (Pissevache).
**Glacier garden** (Gletschergarten) in Zermatt.
**Earth pyramids** at Euseigne.
**Dams** of Mattmark, Moiry, Dixence, Mauvoisin and Emosson.
**Mineral collections and geological exhibitions** on the Grimsel pass, in Binn, Kippel, (lead mine), Zinal, (copper mine), Les Haudères and on the Col de Montets.
**Botanical gardens** in Champex and Bourg St. Pierre and on the Col des Montets (road to Chamonix).
**Alpine zoo** in Les Marécottes.
**Museums:** with a lot of knowledge and attention to detail, many villages in the last few years have set up museums of local culture and they are not dusty piles of junk from the past, but higly interesting collections and lavishly restored tools, houses or barns. In this region of extremes, especially in the once isolated side valleys, there's now a healthy respect for the achievements of earlier generations. Only a limited selection can be mentioned here: Binn, Brig, Kippel, Eggernerg, Saas Fee, Törbel, Sion, Praz-de-Fort.
**Alpine meadow museums** (cheese making exhibitions) and alpine meadow guided tours in Riederalp / Bettmeralp, Nax, Ovronnaz.
**Alpine museums** in Zermatt, Bern and Chamonix.
**Archaeolgical museum** in Martigny.
**Natural history museum** in Sion.
**Wine museum** in Sierre. Visits to wine cellars, with wine-tastings and shops in most of the wine areas.
**Car museum** in Martigny.

Many villages also organise events (concerts, lectures, excursions), and there are open-air plays and festivals. There are all sorts of village festivals, processions, mountain guide festivals, alpine meadow parades and shepherds' feasts. There's cow fighting too. These are bloodless cow fights with folk festival characters where the strongest cow becomes queen. This title accompanied by prizes and prestige for the owner, and respect for the cow from her stall- and meadow-companions.

Also recommended, due to the excellent transport connections, are trips into the neighbouring countries or cantons:
- over the Nufenen pass into the Tessin (post bus).
- over the Furka pass to Andermatt (FO railway)
- over the Grimsel pass to Meiringen and to the Brienzer lake (post bus)
- through the Lötschberg to Thuner lake and to Bern (BLS railway)
- over the Simplon pass to Domodossola, to Lago Maggiore and Lago d'Orta (BLS railway, post bus)
- over the Grand Saint Bernard (or through it) to Aosta (MO bus)
- over the Col de la Forclaz/Montets to Chamonix (MC railway)
- to Geneva lake (SBB).

## Important telephone numbers

**Swiss tourist office:**
the following free telephone numbers are from anywhere in Europe:

| | |
|---|---|
| Tel: | 0080010020030 |
| Fax | 0080010020031 |
| | |
| Valais Tourist Board, Sion: | 027/3273570 |
| Weather report: | 0041/1/162 |
| Internet: | www.MySwitzerland.com |
| | www.wallis.ch |

**NB:** in Switzerland you must dial the local code (even when you are in the area)!

*Looking from the path to the Prabé towards Sanetsch pass (Walk 18).*

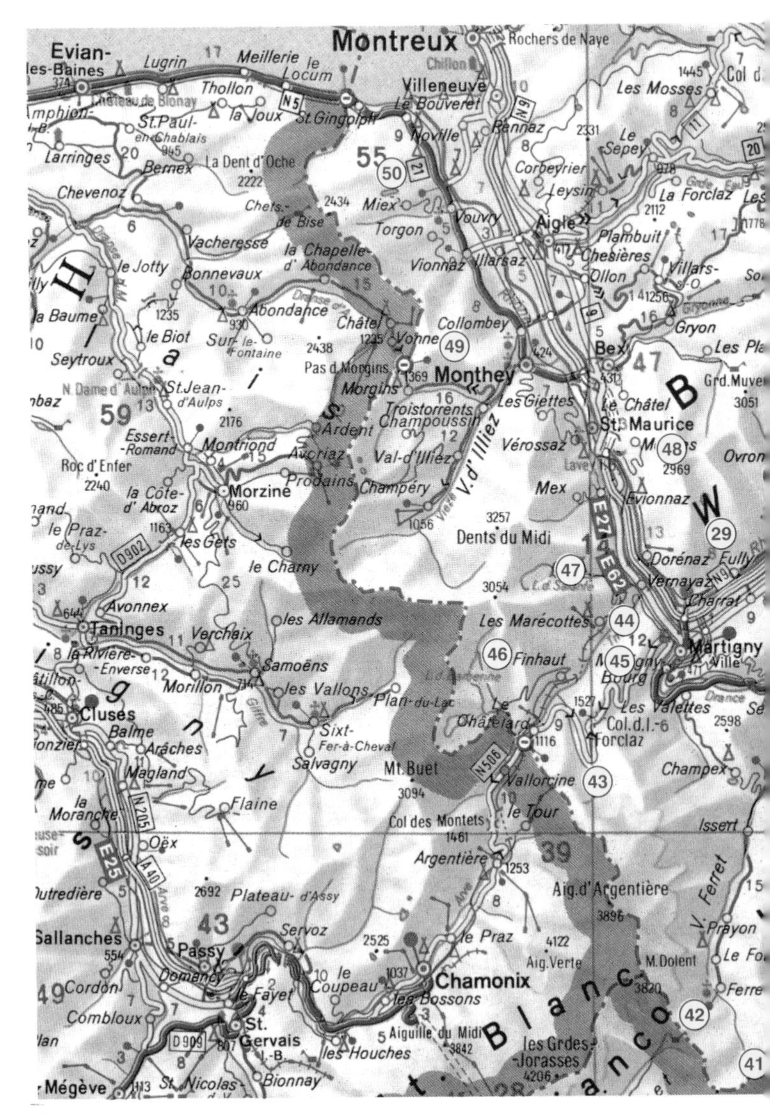
Montreux
Evian-les-Baines
Lugrin
Meillerie
Thollon
St.Gingolph
Villeneuve
Le Bouveret
Rochers de Naye
Les Mosses
Aigle
Monthey
Bex
St.Maurice
Morzine
Châtel
Champéry
Dents du Midi
Martigny
Samoëns
Cluses
Taninges
Sallanches
Chamonix
St. Gervais
Mégève
Argentière
Vallorcine
Finhaut
Les Marécottes
Aiguille du Midi
Mt.Buet
Col des Montets
Champex
Les Grdes Jorasses

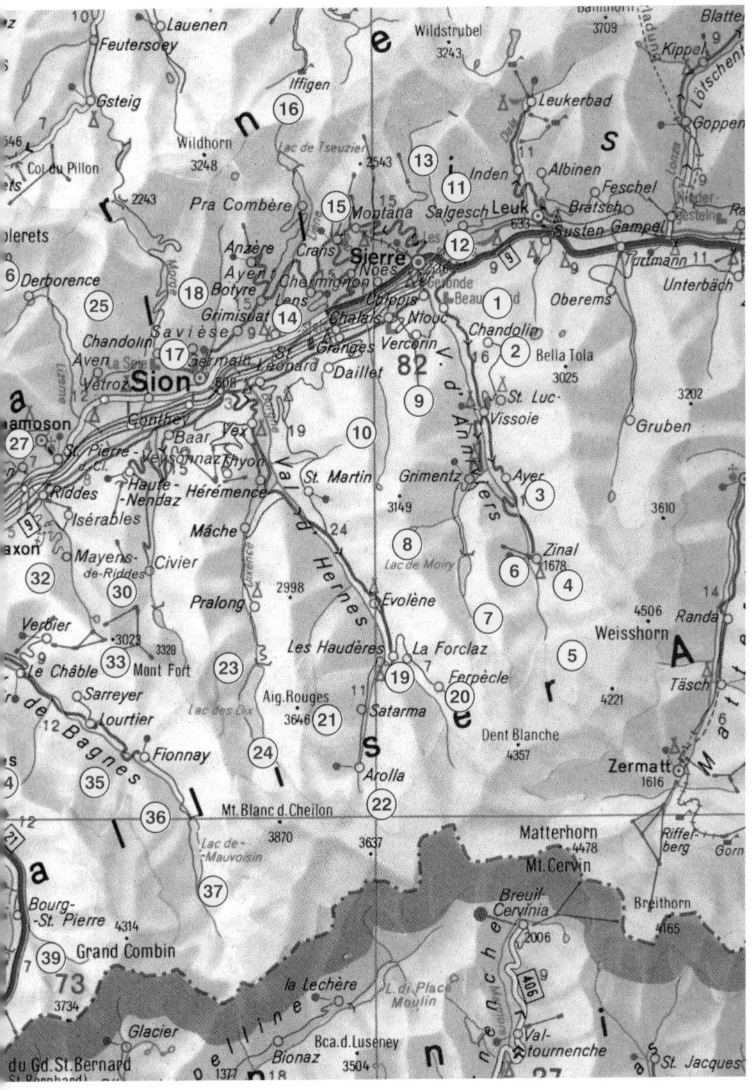

Lauenen
Feutersoey
Gsteig
Col du Pillon
Wildhorn
3248
Wildstrubel
3243
Iffigen
Leukerbad
Inden
Albinen
Feschel
Leuk
Salgesch
Montana
Crans
Sierre
Pra Combère
Anzère
Ayent
Botyre
Chermignon
Lens
Noës
Chippis
Chalais
Niouc
Grimisuat
Savièse
Chandolin
Sion
St. Germain
St. Léonard
Granges
Vercorin
Daillet
Derborence
Vétroz
Conthey
Baar
Vex
Thyon
Riddes
Haute-Nendaz
Hérémence
Isérables
St. Martin
Grimentz
Ayer
Vissoie
St. Luc
Bella Tola
3025
Chandolin
Oberems
Gruben
Turtmann
Unterbäch
Susten
Gampel
Bratsch
Goppenstein
Kippel
Blatten
Mâche
Mayens-de-Riddes
Civier
Pralong
Verbier
Le Châble
Mont Fort
Sarreyer
Lourtier
Fionnay
Val de Bagnes
Evolène
Val d'Hérens
Val d'Anniviers
Les Haudères
La Forclaz
Ferpècle
Satarma
Aig. Rouges
3646
Lac des Dix
Lac de Moiry
Zinal
1678
Weisshorn
4506
Randa
Täsch
Zermatt
1616
Dent Blanche
4357
Arolla
Mt. Blanc d. Cheilon
3870
3637
Lac de Mauvoisin
Matterhorn
4478
Mt. Cervin
Breuil-Cervinia
2006
Breithorn
4165
Riffelberg
Bourg-St. Pierre
4314
Grand Combin
3734
la Lechère
L. di Place Moulin
Glacier
du Gd. St. Bernard
Bca. d. Luseney
Bionaz
3504
Valtournenche
St. Jacques

# 1 Gorwetsch ridge, 2093m

Round path to the Illgraben, the wildest rift valley system in the Alps

## Soussillon – Gorwetsch ridge – Chandolin – Soussillon

**Location:** Sierre, 540m, railway station, bus into Val d'Anniviers; 3km to Niouc, 902m, a tarmac road turns off to Soussillon.
**Starting point:** Soussillon, 1388m, a hamlet which only consists of chalets. Hardly anywhere to park in the hamlet itself so it's best to park the car at the side of the road before the first houses.
**Walking times:** ascent to the Gorwetsch ridge 2¼ hrs., descent to Chandolin ¾ hrs., further descent to Soussillon 1 hrs.; total time 4 hrs.
**Difference in height:** 690m.
**Highest point:** edge of the Illgraben on the Gorwetsch ridge, about 2060m, a little south of the 2093m point.
**Grade:** not very difficult walk, but requires some route finding and surefootedness.
**Food and accommodation:** in the various guest houses in Chandolin.
**Worth seeing:** the view down into the enormous, barren Illgraben, a relic from the Ice Age. The erosion of huge masses of glacial drift and loose rubble has created this rift valley.

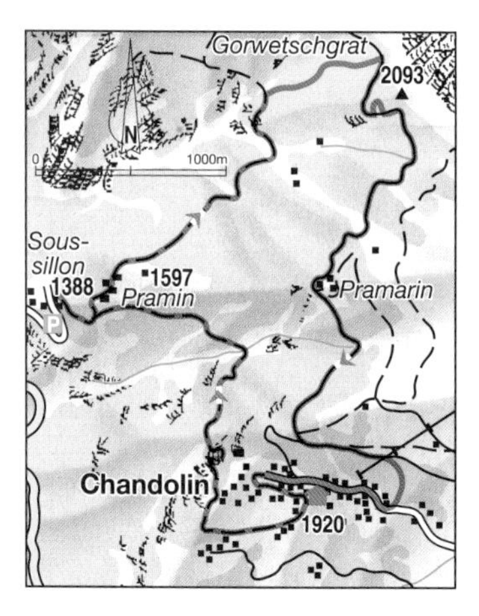


The walk goes repeatedly through the wood in the outer part of Val d'Anniviers and gives you many amazing views into the distance and down into the valley. It is designed as a round walk and so provides new impressions with every step. Together with the view into the Illgraben the descent from Chandolin to Soussillon is also worth a mention. The descent is along a delightful old mountain path, but it has fallen into disrepair enthough you can see that it was once often used.

In **Soussillon** at a pole in the middle of the hamlet go up to the right and onto a footpath which ascends again to the right. After 15 mins. you reach a fork: right goes to Chandolin, but you keep to the left up to the Pramin alp, 1597m (15 minutes). Cross left in front it and without gaining any real height go for about ½ hour through a wood across the slope. The path eventually turns into a narrow path before rather infrequent blue waymarkers lead steeply up in a little valley to a forest road. Follow these to the right in a light larch wood (south); after two zigzags a path turns off left which after only a 25m gain in height on the **Gorwetsch ridge**, reaches the precipice into the

*View across the Illgraben of the Gorwetsch ridge with the Balmhorn behind.*

Illgraben – about 30m below the highest point of the ridge.
Tremendous views down into the desolate cleft await you there and pretty views out towards the Bernese Alps towering up on the far side of the Rhône. Back on the road proceed across a gentle incline to **Chandolin**. After you have passed the lift station go downhill to reach the church and below to the north-west you come to a fork in the path: left goes to Fang, right to Soussillon. This old path descends across steep flanks, crossing some rock steps till eventually, below the Pramin alp, it joins the path you started on and brings you back to **Soussillon**.

# 2 Illhorn, 2717m

High above the primeval Illgraben

## Chandolin – Cabane d'Illhorn – Illhorn – Chandolin

**Location:** Sierre, 540m, railway station, bus into Val d'Anniviers and to Chandolin.
**Starting point:** Chandolin, 1920m, highest village with a church in the Valais which you can drive to from Sierre on a good road through Val d'Anniviers (turn off left in Vissoie). Numerous places to park, but best of all at the valley station for the cable car, 1979m.
**Walking times:** Chandolin – Illhorn 2½ hrs., descent, 1½ hrs.; total time 4 hrs.
**Difference in height:** 800m.
**Grade:** easy walk on marked paths.
**Food and accommodation:** in the Cabane d'Illhorn, 2130m, and in Chandolin.
**Worth seeing:** the Illhorn, a prominent mountain, 2000 metres above the Rhône valley, affords a magnificent view of the Valais and Bernese Alps as well as into the valleys – but especially into the unique Illgraben. The picturesque Illsee lies embedded below the summit in the south-east.

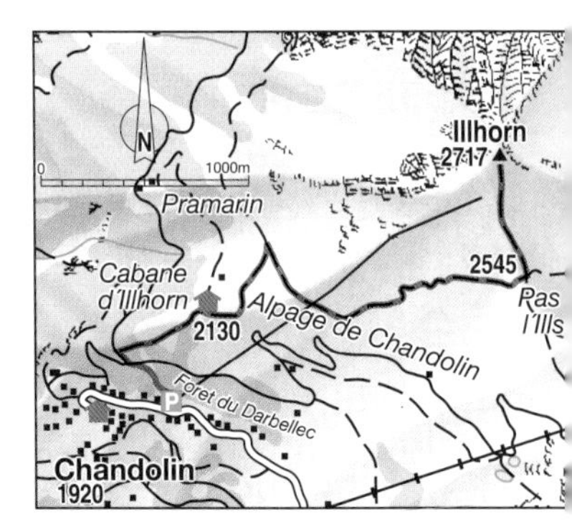


The ascent of Chandolin to the Illhorn across the sunny south-western slopes could be an intensifying experience in itself, since the view gets better with every step – if it wasn't for the ski developments. The narrow path goes repeatedly across the treeless slopes on roads and tracks and past lift pylons as well. The answer to the legitimate question why such a walk is included in our guide, is as follows: because of the totally unparalleled panorama and an incomparable view down the slopes.

Go from the car park in **Chandolin** to the cable car building and up to the right behind it to the start of the track. At first in the wood you gain height until a path turns off right to the **Cabane d'Illhorn**. The path goes through a thin larch and stone pine wood. Go past the hut and along a small path north-eastwards up across the wide slopes of the Alpage de Chandolin. Later continue eastwards, under the cable of the lift going up to the summit, surrounded by the scars in the landscape of the downhill ski runs. For about 2350m you now head directly to the east and to the deepest point of the ridge, to the Pas de l'Illsee, 2545m (not to be confused with the Illpass, 2482m, which lies about a kilometre further to the south-east). Now go due north along the grassy ridge up to the summit of the **Illhorn** which is split in two by a narrow cleft.

Here you can enjoy the famous view of the chain of peaks of the Bernese Alps with the Bietschhorn peak standing supreme; the Weisshorn, Obergabelhorn and Matterhorn dominate the scene in the south and you can just see the Mont Blanc massif in the west, with the summit of the Dents du Midi on the right. But an extraordinary view presents itself of the remote, almost vegetation-free Illgraben with a drop of over 2000 vertical metres. Go back to **Chandolin** the way you came.

*View of the Bella Tola from the Illhorn after the first fall of snow in autumn.*

# 3 St. Luc – Zinal mountain path

Varied walk high above Val d'Anniviers

## St. Luc – Prilett – Nava Secca alp – Zinal

**Location**: Vissoie, 1204m; central place in the valley, turn-off to Zinal and Grimentz (Val de Moiry). Post bus service to Sierre (about 7 buses a day, a good 30 min. journey, 21km).
**Starting point:** St. Luc, 1655m; holiday village on a high terrace, funicular railway to the Bella Tola. Buses to Vissoie (7 a day, 15 min. journey, 8km). Parking places at the penultimate bend below the village (sign: 'Ayer') a few metres on the right, car park on the left.
**Walking times:** St. Luc – Prilett 40 mins., Prilett – Nava Secca 2 – 2½ hrs., Nava Secca – Zinal 2½ – 3 hrs.; total time 5½–6½ hrs.
**Difference in height:** 560m.
**Highest point:** Barneuza alp, 2211m.
**Grade:** varied walk which requires some stamina.
**Food and accommodation:** Café Prilett, 1692m; hotels and restaurants in Zinal and St. Luc.
**Worth seeing:** in St. Luc: planetary path from Tignousa mountain station to the Hotel Weisshorn. In Ayer below the mountain path Georg Winkler lies hidden on the south side of the church, having plunged to his death on the west face of the Weisshorn. Views into the Zinal basin, beautiful panorama of the Val de Moiry with Grimentz.

A path with lots of new surprises and a constant change of scenery: thin patches of wood with lovely solitary trees along the water channels (Suonen) and alpine pastures with many fabulous views.
From the car park below **St. Luc** go along the road in the direction of Ayer for 15 mins into the dog-leg of the valley. At a water container go steeply left uphill along a path to the Café **Prilett**. Now continue along a new forest road across

*The Zinalrothorn peak dominates the end of the Zinal valley.*

a stream and through the wood to the alpine huts of Gillou, 1823m. Descend to the huts (signpost) and take the upper path gently uphill to the south. The path constantly alternates between woods and open ground. Keep the huts of Les Moyes below on the right as you continue to the **Nava Secca alp**, 2146m. Descend a short way along the narrow forest road and after 5 mins. turn off to the south-east along a pretty path (Navetta hut) to the stream. Go up through green elder bushes to the meadows of Barneuza, and the hut just after that. From here there's a marvellous view into the Zinal basin. Continue in a small valley (water channels) and now turn directly to the south and descend to the 2025m point above Zinal. Down an uninviting eroded path, cross two huge stream dams and continue along the tarmac road to **Zinal.**

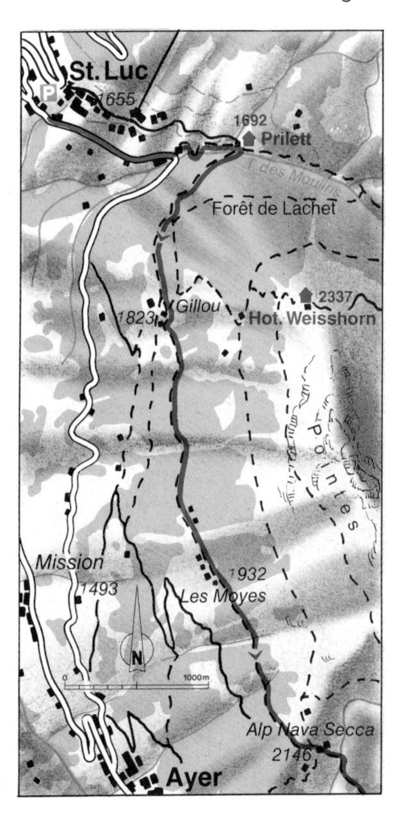


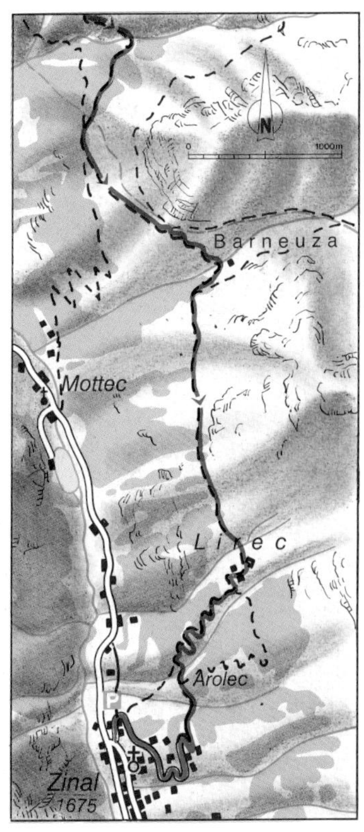

# 4 Roc de la Vache, 2581 m

Belvedere high above the Zinal valley

**Zinal – Combautanna alp – Roc de la Vache – Ar Pitetta – Zinal**

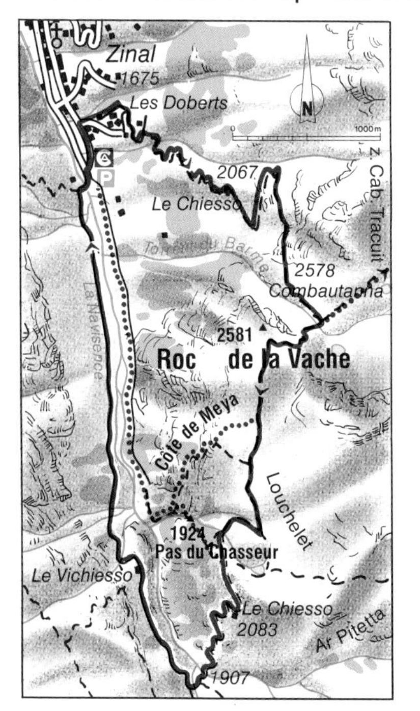


**Location and Starting point:** Zinal, 1675m.
Highest place in Val d'Anniviers. Post bus service to Sierre (about 7 buses a day, about 1¼ hrs. journey, 36km). Places to park at the end of the road south of Zinal; the roadway further up the valley is closed to cars.
**Walking times:** Zinal – Roc de la Vache 3 hrs., descent via Ar Pitetta to the run-off from the Zinal glacier 1¼ hrs., return to Zinal just over 1 hr.; total time, therefore, a good 5 hrs.
**Difference in height:** 900m.
**Grade:** well-made, marked paths posing no problems, although the ground is very steep below the Combautanna. No facilities on the way; however the Petit-Mountet hut can be reached in a good 30 mins. after the run-off from the Zinal glacier (see Walk 5).
**Worth seeing:** the Roc de la Vache is one of the finest vantage points above the Zinal valley. The most impressive views from here are of the dramatically fissured Moming glacier with the pointed Zinalrothorn, the other side of the valley and the north-east flank of the Dent Blanche.

This walk is very rewarding and not too strenuous to do in a day. If, however, you visit the Tracuit hut (SAC hut, staffed in summer) you should take a break, since the last part of the ascent in the heat of the sun on the south slope of the Diablons is like being in an oven (an additional 2 hours ascent).
The turn-off from the valley road at the southern end of **Zinal** village is marked with a sign post; a road winds round bends between newly built houses to the lowest of the foothills of the Tracuit alp (Les Doberts), then a path leads across an avalanche gully and up to Le Chiesso, 2067m.
The ground above now gets steeper and is scattered with rocks, but you reach the Torrent du Barmé round a gentle loop from the left. Where the

*View from Sorebois (Walk 6) of Roc de la Vache (in the middle of the picture) and the Weisshorn chain.*

ground levels out again at the **Combautanna alp**, turn off right from the Tracuit hut path, cross over a stream on a bridge to the south and climb a short way up to the **Roc de la Vache**.

**Descend** via **Ar Pitetta** into the Zinal valley: go due south from the Roc along an obvious path over the sloping meadows to Louchelet and continue downhill via Le Chiesso, 2083m. Eventually round some short bends and through the thin larch wood you reach the splendid confluence of the torrents from the Zinal and Moming glaciers. There's a bridge here across to the other bank where you meet a roadway. This ascends only a bit more to Le Vichiesso and then leads down to the big alluvial plain of La Navisence south of **Zinal** in about 20min.

There are two steep alternatives for descent from the Louchelet area (via Côte de Meya and Pas du Chasseur) directly down to La Navisence. They are quite exposed in places and are only recommended for experienced and sure-footed mountaineers.

# 5 Cabane du Mountet, 2886m

Hut walk into a magnificent glacier basin

**Zinal – Le Vichiesso alp – east bank hut path – Cabane du Mountet – Zinal glacier – west bank hut path – Petit-Mountet hut – Zinal**

**Location and starting point:** Zinal, 1675m; highest village in Val d'Anniviers. Post bus service to Sierre (roughly 7 buses a day, about 1¼ hrs. journey, 36km). Places to park at the end of the road south of Zinal; the roadway further up the valley is closed to cars.
**Walking times:** Zinal – Le Vichiesso ¾ hrs., hut ascent 4 hrs., descent to the Petit-Mountet hut 3 hrs., back to Zinal 1 hr.; total time 8½ – 9 hrs.
**Difference in height:** 1220m.
**Grade:** good, marked path; stamina, sure-footedness and reliable weather important. You have to make a crossing of a glacier on the return: no problems in summer in clear visibility and when the glacier is free of snow, but never go across if the glacier is covered in snow or there's any fog.
**Food and accommodation:** Cabane du Mountet (staffed from July to September, enquire in the valley; telephone for the hut: 027/4751431). Petit-Mountet hut, also staffed from July to September, overnight accommodation possible (tel: 027/475 1380).
**Worth seeing:** the Zinal glacier basin is one of the showpieces of the Valais Alps, not infinitely broad glacial fields as on the Gorner ridge, but a glacial river flowing down over steep ledges with areas of crevices and séracs. This is how you imagine the western Alps, but without the hoards of people at all the famous vantage points.

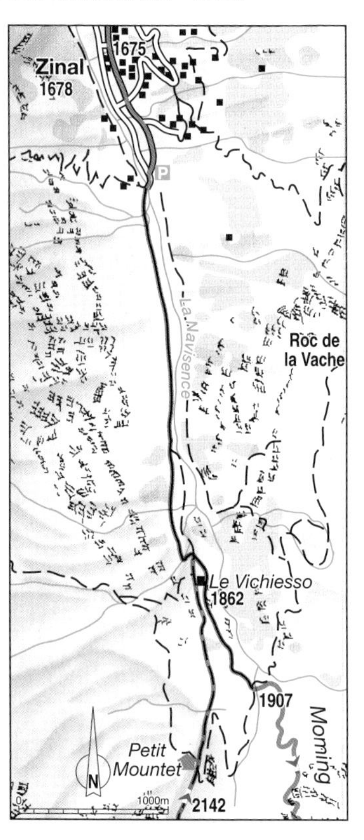


The Cabane du Mountet is situated in a very remote location; it is rarely full since the route to the surrounding four-thousanders is along very demanding paths. For this reason it is highly recommended that you make an overnight stop (but do not forget to telephone beforehand), although staying

overnight in one of these special 'four-thousander huts' can be a more forbidding experience due to the occasionally cramped conditions.
From the car park at the south end of **Zinal** village you go over the bridge and follow the roadway on the west bank of La Navisence to the south as far as the start of the ascent. Stay on the roadway which ascends across the gorge to the **Le Vichiesso alp** (1862m). Shortly afterwards the newly laid Mountet hut path branches off to the right on the west side of the glacier, but you descend along the roadway to the left into the bottom of the valley. Cross the bridge over the run-off from the Zinal glacier and you come to the turn-off towards the Tracuit and Ar-Pitetta huts (about 1½ hrs.). Take the right hand path and wind up the Moming slope in a south-easterly direction. High above the ruptures down to the Zinal glacier, the **east bank hut path** crosses the entire west flank of the Besso on meadows and gravel slopes where you have to cross over some runnels. On the south-west ridge of the Besso climb steeply up again a short way over the area of rocks (cable), then cross boulder fields in a south-easterly direction to the **Cabane du Mountet**.
The time of day and the weather conditions should help you decide whether to descend back down into the valley on the same day or stay overnight in

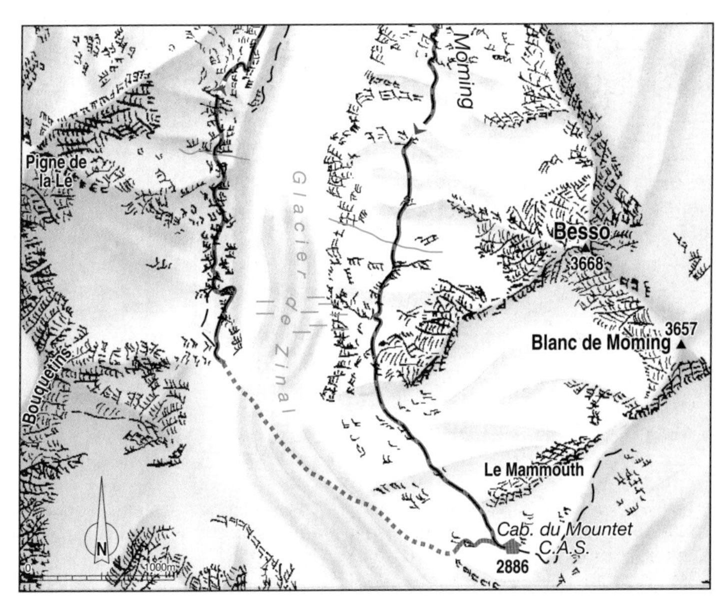

*Inside the Cabane du Mountet where you can prepare a good meal.*

the hut, but for the return you need to reckon on a good 4 hours walking time. Before the descent to the glacier traverse you should enquire at the hut about the conditions, and if there's any doubt you can go back down the ascent path.
Descend steeply down to the west from the hut to the **Zinal glacier** and go leisurely downhill for a good kilometre along the right hand edge; the glacier turns to the right here and forms a large area of crevices. To cross the glacier, keep going in the same direction as before and reach the opposite bank at the end of one of the ribs of rock coming down from the Bouquetins (waymarkers). Then follows an ascent of 150m in altitude along the newly laid **west bank hut path** after the old and lower path was destroyed in places by mudslides and avalanches. Now descend again the slopes below the Pigne de la Lé to the **Petit-Mountet hut** and, after some well-earned refreshment, continue along the good valley path. You meet the ascent path again at Le Vichiesso and return along this to **Zinal**.

*The Obergabelhorn, imposing show piece of the Cabane du Mountet.*

# 6 Sorebois high mountain path

Classic mountain path with splendid views of the four thousanders

## Zinal – Sorebois – Crevache – Petit-Mountet hut – Le Vichiesso alp – Zinal

**Location:** Zinal, 1675m;
post-bus service from Sierre through Val d'Anniviers (roughly 7 buses a day, about 1¼ hrs. journey, 36km).
**Starting point:** Sorebois, 2438m; mountain station of the Zinal cable car, very popular and much-visited; starting point for paragliders and parapenters. Places to park at the valley station.
**Walking times:** mountain station – Petit-Mountet hut 2½ – 3 hrs., Petit-Mountet hut – Zinal 1 hr.; total time 3½ – 4 hrs.
**Highest point:** 2580m, about mid-way along the path.
**Grade:** easy walk on a well-made path, at first on the level and with only negligible variation in height, more of an incline later and a totally flat walk to finish with along the Navisence valley floor.
**Food and accommodation:** Sorebois mountain station; Petit-Mountet hut.
**Worth seeing:** views of the west sides of the Weisshorn and Zinalrothorn, see also picture on p. 41, as well as of the Obergabelhorn, Matterhorn and Dent Blanche. Ice masses covered in debris on the Zinal glacier which is no longer advancing. Navisence gorge. Starting point for paragliders on Sorebois.

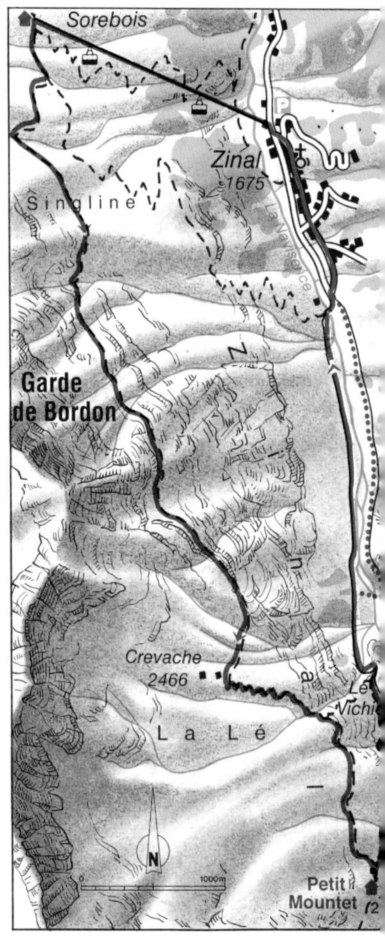


The Zinal basin is one of the show pieces of the Alps because of the four thousanders surrounding it. Zinal is the starting point for the walk to the Tracuit, Ar Pitetta and Mountet SAC-huts, set in magnificent locations.

From the **Sorebois** mountain station of the cable car go southwards across meadows, over some ski slo-

*The glacial run-offs cascade down thundering waterfalls into the Navisence valley.*

pes, into the Torrent des Rochers valley. Continue through the wonderful high mountain scenery below the Garde de Bordon – following numerous clefts and fields of debris – towards the big meadow areas of **Crevache**, 2466m: a very beautiful place to stop for a rest with an amazing panorama. The steep and poor path starts here down to the 2240m point. Do not descend left at the fork there directly into the bottom of the valley, but keep right towards the **Petit-Mountet hut**, 2142m, which you finally reach after a short ascent.
**Return:** either along the newly laid supply channel or along the beautiful path through the wood to **Le Vichiesso alp**. Now descend to the valley floor and continue along the roadway on the left or the right hand side of La Navisence to **Zinal**.

# 7 Cabane de Moiry, 2825m

High mountain hut with surprisingly easy access

## Lac de Moiry – Cabane de Moiry

**Location:** Grimentz, 1564m; for more detailed information see Walk 8.
**Starting point:** Moiry reservoir, a good road goes from Grimentz up to the top of the Lac de Moiry dam, then along the east bank and on to the car park at the upper glacial lake at 2350m. Post bus service from Grimentz between about 9.00 and 17.00. The road is kept open after the snow clearance in June until the first falls of snow in the autumn.
**Walking times:** ascent to the hut from the end of the road 1¾ hrs., return 1 hr.; total time: 2¾ hrs.
**Difference in height:** 480m.
**Grade:** good, marked mountain path.
**Food and accommodation:** restaurant at the top of the dam, staffed as long as the road is open. Cabane de Moiry, SAC, staffed from the beginning / middle of July to the middle / end of September (enquire in the valley), about 90 overnight places, tel: 027/2831018.
**Worth seeing:** Grimentz and Lac de Moiry; spectacular views of the Moiry glacier which flows in several tiers to the reservoir; an especially good view of the ice face of the Pointes de Mourti.

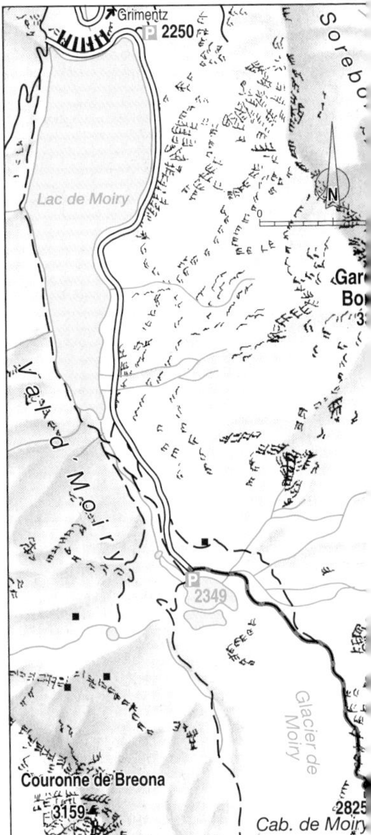

After Dixence, Mauvoisin and Mattmark the **Lac de Moiry** is the fourth biggest reservoir on the Swiss side of the Valais Alps.
Water power is one of the cleanest forms of energy production – but not without making some intruscous into nature. Holidaymakers also profit from these constructions, as certain high mountain valleys would otherwise not be so easily accessible.
At the car park with the small kiosk follow the broad path which ascends the

east side of the lake and leads across gently hilly meadows to the ridge of moraine at the Moiry glacier. Stay only briefly on the increasingly knife-edge ridge, then the path crosses a small valley and leads directly up beside the rocks to the sudden steep rise in terrain. The hut stands on the upper ledge and has been visible from the beginning of the walk. Climb up round innumerable zigzags, but more quickly than you would expect, to the **Cabane de Moiry**.

Unfortunately you cannot walk from the hut since all the surrounding peaks can only be reached over rocks and ice; but you can climb up the little path for a few metres across the steep flank to the glacier to get a closer look at the crevices.

The return is back down the same way.

There are alternatives across the glacier for sure-footed walkers and only when the glacier is clear and there's good visibility: a small path goes from the hut due west down to the glacier. Lower down you have to wangle your way between large boulders in places across the last few metres of the very steep moraine slope to the edge of the glacier. (Be careful not to knock any stones down if there are people below!). Cross over the glacier in a straight line to the opposite bank where there are a few crevices. Then follow some tracks to the moraine ridge and on a good path head up the valley. In the lower section you come through a beautiful little morainal valley.

*Views of Grand Cornier and Dent Blanche across the Lac de Moiry.*

# 8 Sasseneire, 3254m

High view point between Val d'Anniviers (Moiry) and Val d'Hérens

## Lac de Moiry – Alpage de Torrent – Col de Torrent – Sasseneire

**Location:** Grimentz, 1564m; situated at the start of Val de Moiry a little above the turn-off from Val de Zinal. Post bus service to Sierre via Vissoie (7 buses a day, journey lasts about 1 hr., 31km), also a shuttle bus travels in high summer between Vervorin, Vissoie, Grimentz and Zinal.
**Starting point:** Lac de Moiry, top of the dam, 2250m; a good road goes up from Grimentz; post bus between about 9.00 and 17.00). Parking places at the top of the dam.
**Walking times:** Lac de Moiry – Alpage de Torrent 40 mins.; Alpage – Col de Torrent 2 hrs., summit ascent 1 hr.; total time 3½ – 4 hrs.; return 2½ hrs.; total time 6 – 6½ hrs.
**Difference in height:** 1010m.
**Grade:** easy mountain walk on good, not too steep paths as far as the Col de Torrent. The summit ascent should only be undertaken by sure-footed mountaineers and in good weather conditions.
**Food and accommodation:** restaurant at Lac de Moiry (open in summer).
**Worth seeing:** Grimentz, a typical and especially well-kept Valaisan mountain village.
Lac de Moiry: not as big as its western neighbours (Dix- and Mauvoisin reservoirs), but nevertheless very impressive with its 150m high dam which is almost vertical at the top. Beautiful view across the lake of the Moiry glacier and the surrounding peaks. The Sasseneire affords an open panorama across the whole of the western Valais and the Bernese Alps.

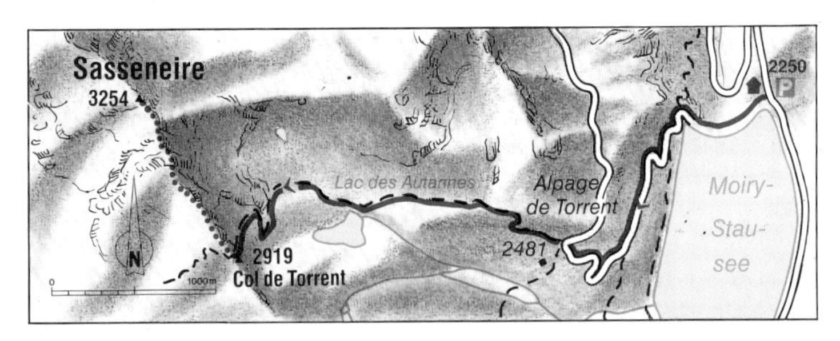


Even without the summit ascent this walk is a very rewarding one and the Col de Torrent gives you a surprisingly good panorama. You can continue this walk with a descent from the Col to Villa above Evolène, where there's a very good path here too.
Ascent to the Col de Torrent: from the car park at **Lac de Moiry** cross the dam to the west where a small roadway winds up to the Moiry pastures and the **Alpage de Torrent**, 2481m.
The roadway now continues to the north to the Basset de Lona, but a

*The glacial mountains around the Moiry hut tower up above Lac des Autannes.*

signpost indicates the path to the Col de Torrent which gently ascends across the grasslands to the marvellous Lac des Autannes. After crossing this small plain the path now ascends round two distinct hairpin bends up to the **Col de Torrent**, 2919m.
Summit ascent to the Sasseneire: tracks run uphill along the west side of the crest of the ridge rather tiresomely across scree and around some small ridge crags – you can walk along tracks on the ridge too, although it means a descent over a three metre high rocky ledge (easy scrambling, grade I). The obvious tracks continue without any further problems over scree to **Sasseneire**.
The **descent** is back the same way.

# 9 Val de Réchy

Peaceful side valley with marvellous water channels near Vercc

## Crêt du Midi – L'Ar du Tsan – Val de Réchy – Vercorin

**Location:** Vercorin, 132 m. Road and cable car link from Chalais (Rhône valley), half-hourly to quarter-hourly between about 6.30 and 21.30.
**Starting point:** Crêt du Midi, 2331m, station for the cable car from Vercorin via Sigeroula.
**Walking times:** Crêt du Midi – L'Ar du Tsan 1 hr., descent into Val de Réchy (La Lé) ¾ hrs., return along the water channel to Vercorin 1½ hrs.; total time 3¼ hrs.
**Highest point:** Crêt du Midi, 2331m.
**Grade:** good hiking paths except for the very first section, sometimes on alpine meadow roads too.
**Food and accommodation:** summit station at Crêt du Midi. No facilities on the way.
**Worth seeing:** pretty panorama from the Crêt du Midi of the Weisshorn and the Bernese Alps across the Rhône valley. A little less pleasant are the unmistakable scars of the ski development opposite which spoil the landscape in Crans-Montana. It was built on the occasion of the world ski championship 1987 – is this really the only possible chance of survival for the people who live in the village? Vercorin has, at any rate, chosen another way: no great development of the lift area and the establishment of Val de Réchy as a nature reserve.

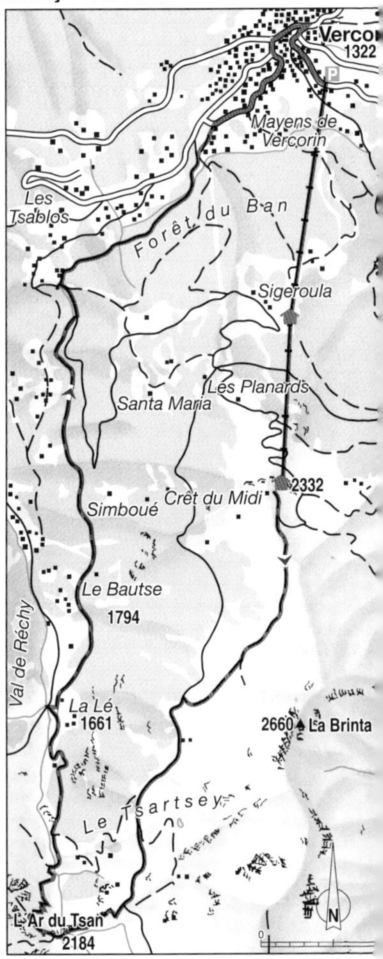


Of course you don't have to take the cable car up to the **Crêt du Midi**, but if you don't, there's an ascent of 1000m in altitude which is partly across the skiing area; the additional good 3 hours make a strenuous mountain hike out of a comfortable walk. Proceed from the summit station a few metres to the south onto a small col.

*A treasure in modern times: a streaming running wild, left unrestrained in Val de Rechy is not built-up.*

Leave the ridge which continues to La Brinta and descend gently to the right close to the tree boundary across to an alpine road. Continue up the valley almost totally on the level until you reach the strangely sheer edge of the marshy basin of **L'Ar du Tsan**. The road leads further up the valley, but you descend to the run-off from the plateau where you find a pretty waterfall surrounded by interesting flora.
For the **descent** cross to the other side just for a short way on the level along the valley. Then the path winds steeply down across the alder-covered slope into the valley bottom and continues, close to the foaming water, to the small alp of La Lé (1661m) in the **Val de Réchy**. The water channel begins here and mainly in the wood, the very gentle path leads beside it out onto the ridge of Les Tsáblos; there you meet the first houses of **Vercorin**. At first through the wood, walk the last two kilometres directly down to the village.

# 10 Mont Noble, 2673m

A high outpost at the start of Val d'Hérens

**Mase – La Combe alp – Col de Cou – Mont Noble – La Combe – Mase**

**Location and starting point:** Mase, 1345m.
Good bus service to Sion, about 6 buses a day with a journey of nearly 40 mins., but it's sensible to hire a car or take a taxi since the starting point lies a bit further up. Parking places at the end of the alpine meadow road (no entry sign) to La Louère (about 2000m).
**Walking times:** ascent to La Combe alp ¾ hrs. (from Mase it's 1½ hrs. longer), onward path to the Col de Cou ¾ hrs. and to the summit ½ hr.; descent about 1 hr. (to Mase 2 hrs.); total time 3 hrs. or 5 – 6 hrs.
**Difference in height:** 680m.
**Grade:** good, marked paths.
**Food and accommodation:** only in Mase, no facilities on the way.
**Worth seeing:** beautiful panorama across the Rhône valley of the Bernese Alps and into Val d'Hérens as well as the quiet Val de Réchy; the summit is adorned with a large statue.

Mont Noble has not yet met with the fate of its neighbours, thank goodness, by which, in the French style, hardly a slope in the region of the 'Quatre Vallées' has been left untouched and hardly a village has been preserved in its traditional style. There, a skier's dream turns into a hiker's nightmare every summer. At least the beautifully situated villages of Nax, Vernamiège and Mase are still what every holidaymaker could wish for. You can still find peace on Mont Noble, the railway lines from Nax end 300m below the summit and the building sins of the alpine road planner are still being kept relatively contained. However, as it's not only a few privileged persons who might travel here, these constructions can spare you a few hours of ascent and descent. Although the road from **Mase** still goes a little further up, it's recommended that, before the turn-off to the high barbecue site ('Feuerstelle'), you drive along a roadway as far as the stream bed (barrier, parking places).

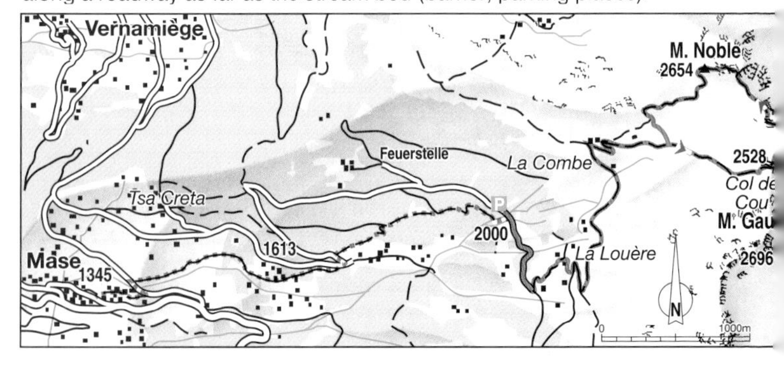

*From Mont Noble you can see the Weisshorn in the east across Val de Rechy.*

Continue along the roadway on open ground until after about 400m just before the crossing of the third gully, the footpath turns off left to La Louère meadows. Cross over to the left above these to **La Combe alp** (2324m). From here go quite steeply uphill along a good path across meadows to the Col de Cou, where the first views emerge down into the upper Val de Réchy. The path now runs across the more and more sparsely covered meadows keeping close to the ridge, with rock precipices into the Val de Réchy on the right, to **Mont Noble**. Before you go over to the western summit with the statue of the Madonna, you should take time to enjoy the incredible views into Val de Réchy from this highest point, and from the statue itself the view is then open to the west.
The descent now goes across the western and southern grass-covered slopes directly back to **La Combe** and from here along the ascent path via La Louère to the car.

# 11 Bisse de Varen

Contrasting programme: open water channels on extremely dry slopes

**Miège – La Proprija alp – Bisse de Varen – Brand – Varen**

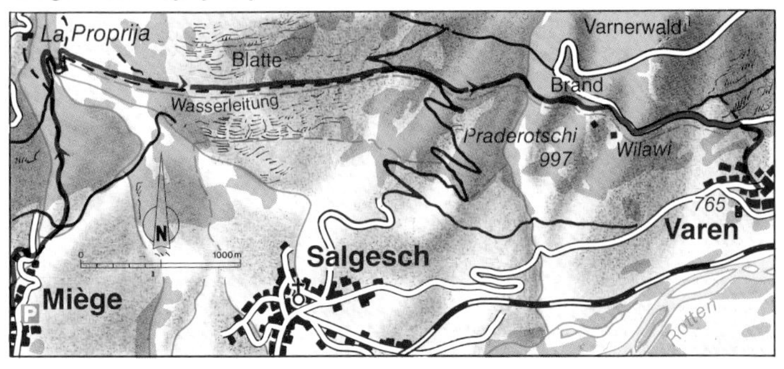


**Location:** Sierre, 540m; small town in middle Valais on the language boundary. IC railway station.
**Starting point:** Miège, 702m; pretty wine village a little way off the road leading from Sierre to Montana. Buses with frequent service to both places.
**Destination:** Varen, 760m; also in the middle of vineyards on a small terrace, just above the first rocky ledge over the Rhône valley. Buses to Sierre.
**Walking times:** Miège – La Proprija 1 hr., Bisse de Varen – Brand 1¼ hrs., descent to Varen ½ hr.; total time 2¾ hrs.
**Difference in height:** 280m.
**Highest point:** on the Bisse de Varen, about 1040m.
**Grade:** easy walk.
**Food and accommodation:** guest houses in Miège and Varen.
**Worth seeing:** vineyards near Miège, interesting stands of pine trees in extremely dry locations on the ascent. The water channel ('Bisse') seems more like a stream running across the slope, with dense and lush vegetation flourishing on the otherwise sun-baked southern slope where only drought adapted species survive under the plants. Because of the overgrown vegetation the channel is easily recognisable from a distance as you travel to the Rhône valley.

The ascent is south facing which, on a hot day, can cause you to sweat a little so it's best not to set out too late. The slope which is crossed by the water channel (Blatte) marks the slide of a huge ice-age rock fall from the upper Varneralp; the hilly landscape of Pfyn forest (Walk 12) originated through the sedimentation of debris from the landslide after the retreat of the glacier. Important: please do not alter the position of anything on the water channels, these irrigation channels are still essential to agriculture even in the age of automatic watering systems and an uncontrolled overflow of water

can quickly destroy the embankments.
At the church square in **Miège** (bus stop, signpost) take the little road which runs towards the mountains through the town. At the last houses you come to the vineyards and continue uphill to the wood. The path goes over a small col on the hill of Planigettes and reaches a chapel just below **La Proprija alp**. About 20 meters higher up you come to the **'Bisse de Varen'** water channel which crosses the dry slope for about 2km with the minimal incline. It's as if you are walking here through a tunnel of pines – pleasantly shady and yet with regular views into the Rhône valley and Val d'Anniviers opposite. Finally you enter a dense wood again, cross a small rift valley to **Brand** and shortly after that meet a roadway which leads from Varen into Varner forest.
Descend this roadway for about 1km to just above **Varen** where you find a footpath to take you directly down into the village.

*A tunnel of pines encloses the water channel.*

# 12 Pfyn forest

Nature trail through a landslide area formed by the ice age

**Location:** Sierre, 540m.
**Starting point:** car park at the campsite on the Sierre – Brig canton road, just beyond the Rhône bridge.
**Walking times:** the real walking time on this round walk is hardly 45 minutes, but to fully appreciate the special features of this landscape you should plan at least half a day, if not a whole one.
**Difference in height:** 70m.
**Highest point:** hill in Pfyn forest, about 610m.
**Grade:** easy valley walk, but no facilities on the way.
**Worth seeing:** interesting, varied plant and animal life in the conservation area which is distinguished by the contrast of extreme dryness and boggy dampness. Some species are only found here in Switzerland. Historic buildings in Sierre.

Pfyn forest is the last bit of land which has largely remained unspoiled in the otherwise very intensively exploited upper Rhône valley. The Rhône still flows here along its former bed through the hilly landslide area covered predominantly with pines.
A rock precipice from Varneralp above Salgesch onto the ice-age Rhône glacier lead, after its retreat, (about 10,000 years ago) to the depositation of this hill of debris in the Pfyn-Sierre area. The Swiss environmental organisation (SBN) has been working for years on the realisation of a nature reserve in the Pfyn forest.

*The Rhône at Pfyn has retained its original river bed.*

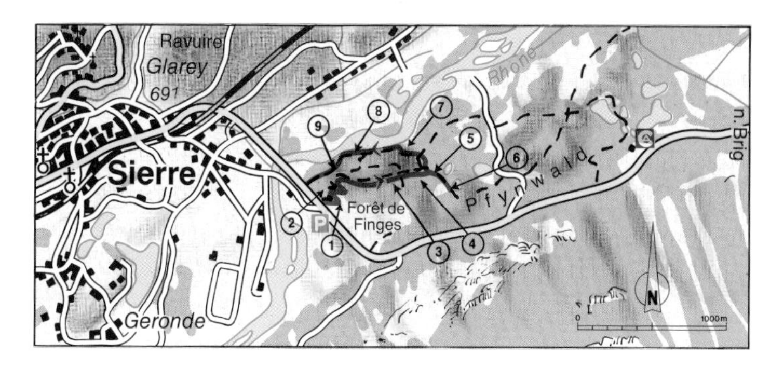


It has published a small guide which contains information about Pfyn and vividly portrays the problems and threats to this place of refuge for rare species (obtainable at the tourist offices of Sierre and Susten, at the campsite or direct from the office at SBN, Postfach 73, 4020 Basel). The numbers in the following text can also be found on the round walk and are described in the SBN guide.

The **nature trail** starts at the car park, just 100m after the campsite at the Rhône bridge on the Sierre – Brig road, where there's also an information board. On the first bends you enter the **dry area** with oddly Mediterranean type plants (1). A little later you asoon find yourself on one of the hills which gives you a good overview of the **dry forest** (2).

Walk eastwards into the **Zwergseggen pine forest**, one of the driest forest types of all (3), before you descend into a hollow – the so-called **Weißseggen pine forest** is here (4) which already has to endure much less extreme conditions. At (5) you can see how trees needing light – for example, the pines – influence their immediate living space and thereby do not leave their 'competitors' much chance of flourishing.

A short detour leads to a **pond** filled with sedimentation (6), which consists only of one remaining stand of reeds; in the Pfyn there are other pretty lakes and ponds which can easily be reached along the paths to the east through the hills. The nature trail now leads to **the high bank of the Rhône** (7); the river is not dammed up here and so divides into several river arms with islands which are sometimes washed over when the river is flooded, unfortunately a very rare sight these days.

The return path goes through an area with **meadow steppes** (8), a type of dry meadow which is heavily repressed by the watering, principally on the vineyard slopes. Finally you should make another detour onto the **shingle banks** of the Rhône (9), before returning past the campsite to the starting point.

# 13 Petit Mont Bonvin – La Tièche

A walk along gurgling water channels

**Petit Mont Bonvin – La Tièche – Bisse de Tsittoret – Cave du Sex – L'Aminona**

**Location:** L'Aminona, 1514m. SMC buses with frequent service Sierre – Montana, from here about 3 times a day to L'Aminona; park at the cable car station.
**Starting point:** cable car mountain station at Petit Mont Bonvin, 2383m.
**Walking times:** Petit Mont Bonvin – La Tièche ¾ hrs., along the Bisse de Tsittoret and descent to L'Aminona 1½ hrs.; total time 2¼ hrs.
**Grade:** good, mostly broad paths.
**Food and accommodation:** summit restaurant at Petit Mont Bonvin, restaurant in L'Aminona.
**Worth seeing:** panorama from Petit Mont Bonvin, in particular in the direction of the Zinal valley, but also down into the Rhône valley. The walk goes over long stretches of a historic water channel which was instrumental in helping the cultivation of the sunny meadows, fields and vineyards further below. The waterfalls on the way are a particular attraction of this channel.

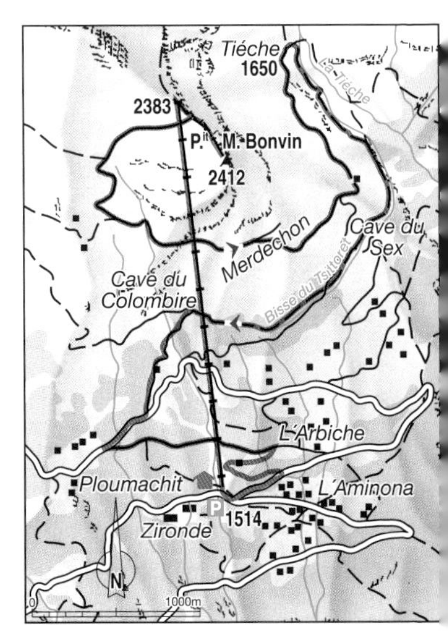


Leave the architectural 'master pieces' of the 'Zironde' high rise complex in L'Aminona with the help of the cable railway and vanish into an area occupied by skiers in winter. If the immediate neighbourhood is not particularly attractive, the distant view of the Valais rocks and icy peaks is certainly one of the finest. You should definitely go over to the summit of **Petit Mont Bonvin** 10 mins. away in any case.
For the descent use the roadway which curves briefly downhill across the skiing area, but then leads to the Merdechon mountain pastures. From the huts of the same name – the roadway turns off left here down into the valley – the path goes almost on the level into the bottom of **La Tièche** valley, where the streams merge from different directions, an ideal play area for children.
Right next to the waterfall descend on the good path with interesting views into the eroded furrow at the start of the **'Bisse du Tsittoret'** water channel; now almost on the level follow the briskly flowing water to the so-called

**Cave du Sex**, where the water passes over another steep ledge with a small waterfall. Here too the path goes down alongside the water over steps, then goes on the level again next to the channel across the slope. Cross over the roadway from Bonvin in the wood, and at the pasture clearing at Cave de Colombire about a kilometre further on, descend again more steeply to the road and along this for a good 500m down to the next pasture clearing (Plumachit), where a signpost points to the turn-off left and back to **L'Aminona** valley station.

*View into the bottom of the Tièche valley with the start of the Bisse du Tsittoret.*

# 14 Le Châtelard, 1272m – Bisse de Lens

Stroll along a water channel to a viewpoint

## Lens – Le Châtelard – Bisse de Lens – Bisse de Silolin – Les Planisses – Chelin

**Location and starting point:** Lens, 1128m; small village on a broad meadow col on the ridge which runs down from Bella Lui towards St. Léonard in the Rhône valley, not far away from the smart sports area of Crans-Montana. Post bus from Sion (almost every hour), local buses from Sierre and Montana (SMC line, about 7 buses a day).
**Destination:** Chelin / Flanthey, about 750m; settlements above the vineyards of St. Léonard – Granges. Postbus from Granges to Lens, about 9 buses a day.
**Walking times:** Lens – Le Châtelard ½ hr., descent to the Bisse de Lens 20mins., Bisse de Lens – Bisse de Silolin to Les Planisses 1¼ hrs., return to Chelin ½ hr. (over the Châtelard back to Lens: 1¼ hrs.); total time 2¼ or 3 hrs.
**Difference in height:** 150m.
**Grade:** easy walk, but a complete lack of vertigo is essential; ideal walk in spring and autumn, but in high summer it can be really hot on the ascent.
**Food and accommodation:** restaurants in Chelin and Lens.
**Worth seeing:** interesting water channels across sheer rock faces.

Beautiful panorama across the Rhône valley from Le Châtelard with its enormous statue of Christ.

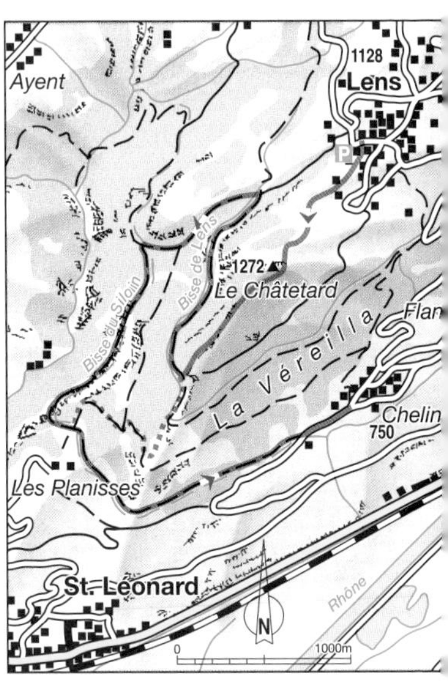


In **Lens** the path begins as a road at the cemetery (car park here too) and leads to the sports field, then continues as a footpath to the wood and as a chapel path to **Le Châtelard** – and at this point all the exertions of the ascent are over.

Descend now across the open south-west ridge with interesting flora to the **Bisse de Lens**; turn right towards Icogne, and follow this water channel (built in the 15th century, no longer in use today) – mainly still in the steep wood at first, then exposed across a rock face – as far as the new tunnel which now channels the water through the mountain to the fields and meadows. Shortly afterwards you come to a roadway and turn off down to the left from the Bisse which continues to Icogne.

*Looking back at the Bisse de Silolin as it crosses the rock face above the Liène gorge.*

Two bends later it descends steeply into the gully; in the meantime a path turns off left to Chelin, but do not take this. In a small forest clearing you come to a fork: the Bisse du Clavau goes to the right towards Icogne and the **Bisse de Silolin** to the left southwards, which quickly leads to a large rock face and becomes very exposed as it crosses the middle of it (cable, lack of vertigo essential); at the ledge the water is channeled over an an artificial waterfall a little away from the path. The path soon gets broader and reaches an edge at **Les Planisses**. Here begin the meadows and vineyards across which the next stage of the path goes beside the flowing water as far as **Chelin**. Return to Lens by bus; or alternatively you can go from Les Planisses along a pretty path back to the upper Bisse de Lens and via le Châtelard to Lens.

# 15 Bisse du Ro

Spectacular water channel near to Crans

## Crans / Plans Mayens – Bisse du Ro – Er de-Chermignon alp

**Location:** Crans, 1476m; with the neighbouring Montana situated on the large terrace above Sierre. Good bus service from both places to Sierre (according to the day and time of day there's a service every half an hour), and funicular railway Sierre-Montana (also leaving about every half hour). Free travel in the Crans – Montana – Vermala area.
**Starting point:** Plans Mayens, 1620m; scattered settlement of holiday chalets north above Crans, bus service (3 times a day).
**Walking times:** about an hour in each direction; total time 2 hrs.
**Highest point:** Er de-Chermignon alp, 1662m.
**Grade:** sometimes very exposed, in places reconstructed water channel path with rope handrail on the rocky sections; only recommended to walkers with a good head for heights.
**Food and accommodation:** restaurant in Plans Mayens. Otherwise no facilities.
**Worth seeing:** the Bisse du Ro is the most daring of all the Valais water channels; it is unbelievable how it crosses such crumbling and exposed rocky flanks – how great the need must have been when it was constructed hundreds of years ago and then had to be maintained under very dangerous and risky conditions.
The most dangerous sections have now been made safe and modern building materials allow the safe crossing of areas where many people once lost their lives. Nevertheless the channel still has to be repaired at great expense every spring or after heavy rainfall; so enquire at the tourist office if there's any doubt.

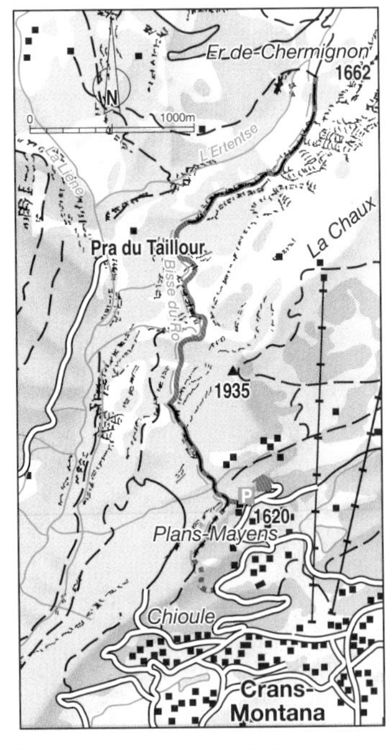


From the 'Beau Cedre' bus stop (there's also a car park here), the last one before the terminus in **Plans Mayens**, descend steeply through dense forest for about 50 vertical metres diagonally down to the water channel. You come to this point from Crans itself if you follow the road to Plans Mayens to the third very wide bend. Go left here (signpost) to reach the start of the

channel (about 45 mins. from Crans, Grand Place). Now the path keeps beside the **Bisse du Ro**, sometimes in the forest, sometimes through the ravine, sometimes across terrifying scree slopes, sometimes across rock faces as an exposed path on the outside of the water channel, then as a broader and more leisurely path again. In several places you should watch your head, as it's possible for not only particularly tall people to collide painfully with the overhanging rocks – not without its dangers considering the narrow path.
After about half way you have an especially beautiful view into the valley of the Lac de Tseuzier (Walk 16), then the path turns into the valley of the Ertentse stream. Here below big rock faces descend into the bottom of the valley as far as the water container below **Er de-Chermignon alp** – on the right above on Bella Lui you can see the cable car installations of Crans-Montana, but they are on the other side of the ridge.
Use the same path for the return, but it gives you totally different views and impressions.

*The Bisse du Ro crosses the rock face with tremendous exposure.*

# 16 Lac de Tseuzier – Rawil pass, 2429m

Ancient pass crossing from the Valais into the Bernese country

## Lac de Tseuzier – Armeillon alp – Rawil pass

**Location:** Ayent, 840 – 1050m; community with several villages above the extensive vineyards at the end of the Liène gorge (at Uvrier – St. Léonard). Post bus service to Sion, frequent buses (about 20 mins. journey, 12km).
**Starting point:** Lac de Tseuzier (barrage du Rawil), 1778m; end of the road from Ayent, post bus terminus (2 buses a day, 35 mins. journey, 20km; just under 1 hour from Sion). Parking at the dam.
**Walking times:** Lac de Tseuzier – Lourantse alpe ½ hr., ascent to Armeillon alp a good ¾ hrs., to the Rawil pass another 1¼ hrs.; total 2½ hrs.; return 1¾ hrs.; total time 4¼ hrs.
**Difference in height:** 750m.
**Grade:** easy walk on good paths, rough forest path as far as Armeillon alp.
**Food and accommodation:** guest house at the dam. No facilities on the way.
**Worth seeing:** the journey up to the reservoir by bus or by car already goes through a marvellous mountain landscape and is an experience in itself. Depending on the level of the water the reservoir displays itself as a pretty blue jewel in the valley or it is enclosed by less beautiful brown banks (early summer). On this walk you cross over several interesting geological layers and experience them at close hand on the excitingly laid forest path. From the top of the pass there's a view into the Bernese Oberland at Lenk.

*View in early summer across the Lac de Tseuzier towards the Rawil pass.*

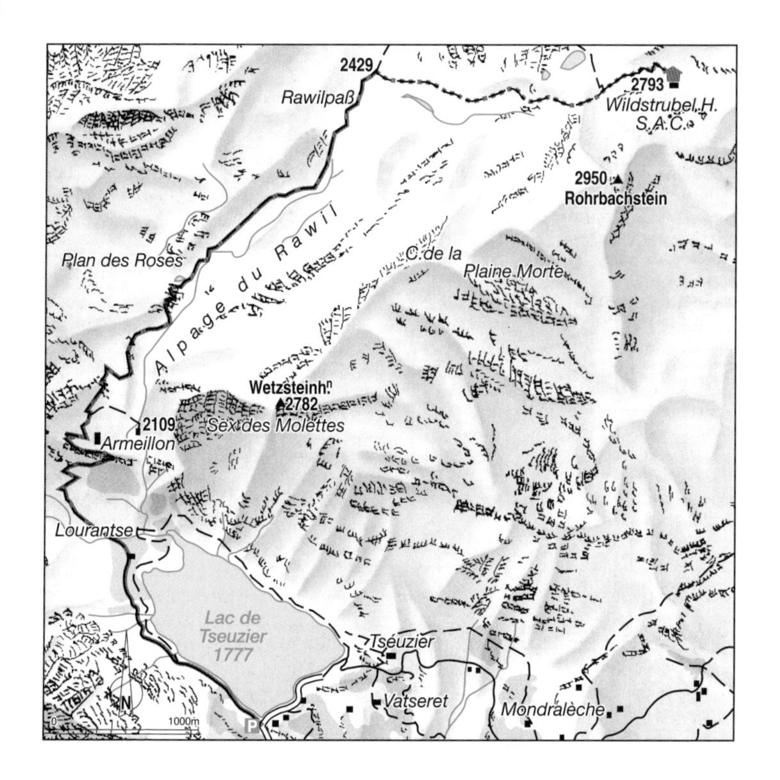


Go along the west bank of the **Lac de Tseuzier** on the roadway to the Lourantse alp, a delightful spot with a marvellous stand of larches surrounded by precipitous flanks. Even if it doesn't seem possible the forest path not only goes up under the barrier of rock, but winds up steeply round hairpin bends until it finally goes through a short tunnel to the small plateau of **Armeillon alp**. There's a magnificent panorama here of the lake and into the Valais. The path now climbs up diagonally to the next sparsely vegetated plateau of Plan des Roses – the name has something to do with the barren soil, not with roses. Now continue on less of an incline in this Nordic-like landscape to the broad **Rawil pass**. – As a bonus you could climb up from the Rawil pass eastwards in about 1 hour along tracks to the Wildstrubel hut (staffed in summer). The return goes back down the ascent path and at the reservoir there's an alternative footpath, only a little longer, on the east side.

# 17 Mont d'Orge, 786m

Short stroll amidst fascinating nature via Sion, capital of the canton

**Lac du Mont d'Orge – Mont d'Orge – Lac du Mont d'Orge**

**Location:** Sion, 500m; capital of the Valais canton, also called the 'wine bar' of Switzerland; Intercity station.
**Starting point:** Lac du Mont d'Orge, 643m, a little south of the road to Savièse in the middle of broad vineyards. Frequent post buses to Sion centre. Accessible on foot from La Planta centry (Office du tourisme, central underground garage) in about 45 minutes.
**Walking times:** Lac du Mont d'Orge – Mont d'Orge 20 mins., descent to the old water channel on the south side 20 mins., return to the Lac du Mont d'Orge 15 mins.; total time 1 hr.
**Difference in height:** 150m.
**Grade:** easy stroll.
**Food and accommodation:** restaurants in Sion.
**Worth seeing:** impressive views down into the Rhône valley and of Sion with its characteristic hills of Tourbillon and Valère, and the vineyards as far as the eye can see. The southern slope above the vineyards is an interesting biotope (you will find cacti amongst other things here and many other Mediterranean plants), in contrast to the primeval forest-type dense undergrowth on the north side. The remains of an old castle stand on the summit. The Lac du Mont d'Orge with its reed-covered banks is a natural jewel.

This short walk is strongly recommended if you are making a quick stop in Sion, and also a tour of the town. It is particularly delightful in late autumn when the vineyards are aglow with warm gold tones and when there's also a good possibility of a clear, distant view of the valley areas.
There are plenty of possible walks, but from the walk described here you can take home with you the most memorable impressions with the least effort.
From Lac du Mont d'Orge go southwards up a gentle incline through the vineyards. Shortly after the last house a zigzag path turns off right (Vita Parcours), which you follow as far as the ruin on the summit of **Mont d'Orge**.

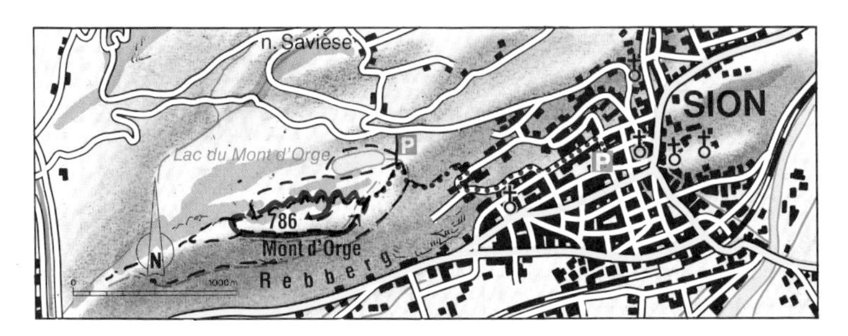

*Vineyards and the hills of Tourbillon and Valère give Sion its character.*

After a few metres along the old ruined walls you reach the highest point with a statue.
First go back down the ascent path to the start of the ruins where the Vita Parcours leads down the north side through the dense wood. You soon meet a roadway along which you walk to the vineyards on a col with beautiful views to the west of the hill. A path runs on the level through the middle of the vines onto the south side of Mont d'Orge and you return to **Lac du Mont d'Orge** along the old water channel (Suone).

# 18 Prabé, 2042m

Stunning views into the distance and down the mountain high above Sion

## Mayens de la Zour – Prabé

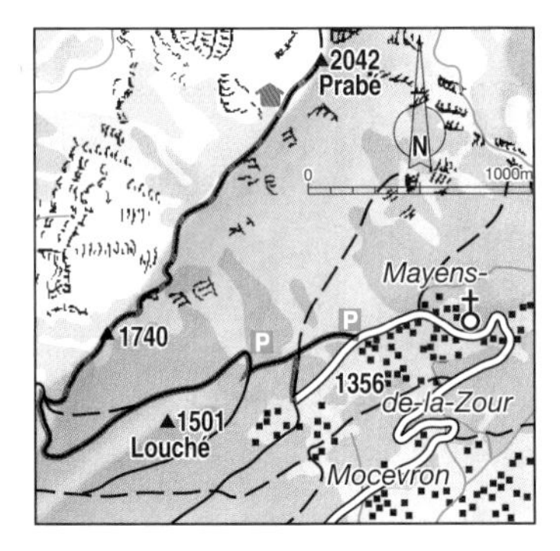


**Location and starting point:** Mayens de la Zour / Prazier, 1343m, former alpine settlement and today's second home and holiday settlement on the sunny slope above Sion-Savièse and the almost unending vineyards. Buses to Sion (about 4 a day, 40 minute journey, 18km). Parking at the bus terminus and at the ascent path which turns off right about 300m before the bus stop and along which you can drive another few metres as far as the no-entry sign.
**Walking times:** 2½ hrs. in ascent, in descent 1½ hrs.; total time 4 hrs.
**Difference in height:** 700m.
**Grade:** good sign-posted path with breath-taking views down onto the steep flanks, rather exposed over some short sections. No facilities; near to the summit there's an un-staffed self-catering hut with overnight accommodation (take your sleeping bag and cooking equipment with you).
**Worth seeing:** its location above the Rhône valley makes the Prabé a superb mountain for views into the valley and of the Valais Alps lined up in the south, and especially of the mountains between the Weisshorn and the Grand Combin over as far as Mont Blanc.
The main part of the ascent runs along the ridge with open views, and there are also impressive views down the very steep scree gullies into the valley leading to the Sanetsch pass.

From the bus terminus in **Mayens de la Zour** go uphill along the narrow path through the wood to the track which you also reach if you go back a good 300m along the road to the bigger junction with signpost. Go uphill along this track in the wood, round two bends and up a pleasant incline onto the mountain ridge which, at the bottom here, is still wooded. Either go round the next hairpin bend or take the shortcut directly to the end of the track and continue uphill along the ridge. It's not much further before you reach the forest boundary and the first open views.
Soon you come to a small upswing where a new path goes on the right across the flank; you can also climb directly over the knife-edged ridge with amazing views down the mountain. Then, quite surprisingly, you meet a pretty meadow, with the steep precipices down to the Rhône on the right and enclosed by a tall forest on the left which lightly covers just as wild and

steep terrain. Continue further along the ridge to the self-catering hut where the view is magnificent. With a few extra metres of ascent to the **Prabé** nearby the panorama gets even better as the view opens up to the east down across horrible terrain covered in loose rocks and scree.
Descend back down the ascent path.

*View from the meadow near the Prabé of its precipitous neighbour, the Pra Roua.*

# 19 Roc Vieux, 2213m

Viewing balcony above Les Haudères

## Les Haudères – Mayens de Veisivi – Roc Vieux

**Location and starting point:** Les Haudères, 1436m; highest village in Val d'Hérens at the fork to Arolla and Ferpècle. Post bus service to Sion (buses about every hour, 50 mins. journey, 37km).
**Walking times:** Les Haudères – Mayens de Veisivi 1¾ hrs., ascent to the Roc Vieux ¾ hrs; return 1½ hrs.; total time 4 hrs.
**Difference in height:** 780m.
**Grade:** not a difficult walk with a broad path at the start (old approach to Arolla), then a good mountain path. No facilities on the way.
**Worth seeing:** extraordinarily rich flora on the meadows above Les Haudères; Roc Vieux offers an excellent overview of the upper Val d'Hérens, crowned with views of Dent Blanche and Pigne d'Arolla.

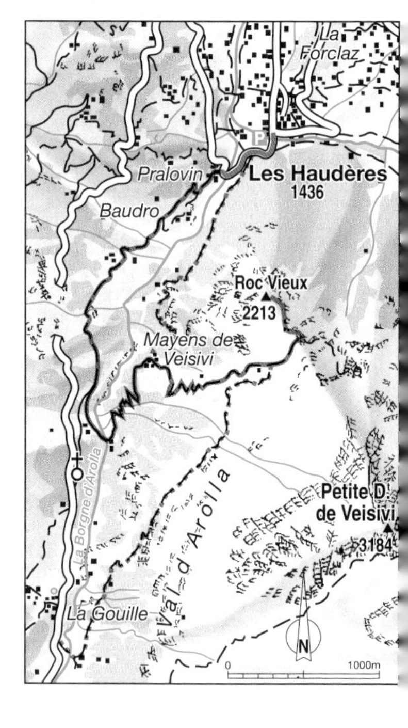


From the post bus stop in **Les Haudères** go along the road to Arolla. First cross the Ferpècle stream, then the Borgne d'Arolla. Leave the road at this point and turn left onto the old path to Arolla which runs up a moderate incline on the left hand side of the stream past the houses of Baudro and La Ventura. The south-east facing slope is open and light in places and covered with meadow plants and bushes. On sunny days countless butterflies frolic here, amongst them Apollo butterflies too. About 500m before the small chapel of St. Barthélemy – a visit here makes for an interesting detour – the path branches off left down to the stream which you cross on a bridge. On the other side of the Borgne the path gets steep and winds up to the **Mayens (summer alpine meadows) de Veisivi**. A small plateau opens out at about 1900m. At the end of the plateau the path ascends another 200m and then leads northwards to the **Roc Vieux** viewpoint. This is situated at an exposed point on the ridge which leads in the other direction up to the Petit Dent de Veisivi.

*Late autumn view from Roc Vieux of the Grand Cornier and Dent Blanche.*

The views of Val d'Hérens in the north, Les Aiguilles Rouges in the west, the ice-covered summits around Arolla in the south and the Dent Blanche with its lesser peaks in the east are stunning and justify the reputation of Roc Vieux as an outstanding viewing balcony above the Evolène valley floor.
If you do not want to go back the same way there's a shorter alternative. At the Mayens de Veisivi branch off right and go steeply up the right hand side of the stream to reach Les Haudères. Another alternative is to descend along a narrow path from above the summer alpine pastures, continue diagonally left to La Gouille on the Arolla road and from here return by bus to Les Haudères. (E. Muscholl / W. Hellberg)

# 20 Bricola alp, 2415m

Wide view of the glacier at the end of the Ferpècle valley

**Salay – Bricola alp – Salay**

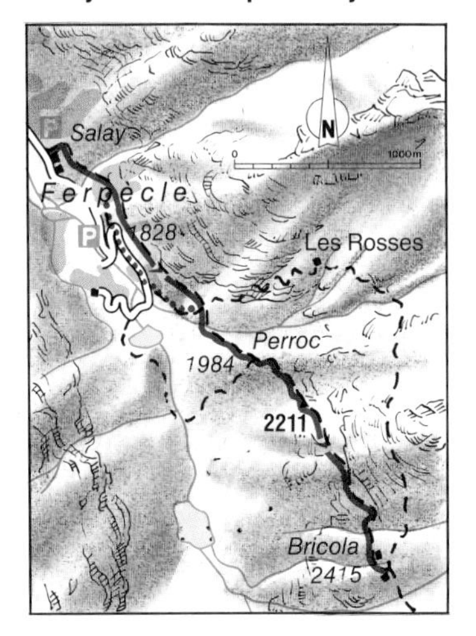


**Location:** Les Haudères, 1436m; situated in Val d'Hérens at the fork to Arolla and Ferpècle.
**Starting point:** Salay, 1766m, in the Ferpècle valley; post bus from Les Haudères (about 4 buses a day between about 8.00 and 17.45, just under 25 mins. journey, 9km). There's limited parking on the road in Salay / Ferècle.
**Walking times:** Salay – Bricola 2¼ hrs.; return 1½ hrs.; total time 3¾ – 4 hrs.
**Difference in height:** 650m.
**Grade:** easy walk on good and adequately marked paths. No facilities.
**Worth seeing:** impressive views of the dramatically fissured glacial tongues from the Ferpècle and Mont Mine glaciers. From Bricola the Dent Blanche displays itself like a massive tooth which lives up to its nickname after a new fall of snow. At other times is nowhere near as white.

For just under half a kilometre follow the little road from **Salay** up the valley (last chance to park for cars) and after another 500m you come to the mountain pastures of Ferpècle.
The good path now climbs south-eastwards across the pastures, zigzags up over a small rock barrier at the 2211m point and then, at a moderate incline, finally leads through two rift valleys troughs to the huts of the **Bricola alp**, 2415m. The contrasts could hardly be greater: the glacial tongues with the huge fields of moraine below, the ice and rock peaks above and this green island of alpine pasture.
Of course you can, if you like, walk up a bit further from Bricola along the path to the Dent Blanche hut across the beautiful Ruisseaux de Bricola pastures from where the views of the wild mountain landscape are even more stunning.
The descent goes back down the ascent path.

*The Dent Blanche looks especially impressive from the Bricola alp.*

# 21 Cabane des Aiguilles Rouges, 2810m

Easy round hut walk in an extraordinarily beautiful landscape

**Arolla – Pra Gra alp – Cabane des Aiguilles Rouges – Lac Bleu – Arolla**

*The Cabane des Aiguilles Rouges, a natural stone building in keeping with the landscape.*

**Location and starting point:** Arolla, 1998m. Bus service to Sion via Evolène and Les Haudères (52km, 1¼ hour journey).
**Walking times:** Arolla – Pra Gra upper alp 1¼ hrs., Pra Gra – Cabane des Aiguilles Rouges 1¼ hrs., descent to Lac Bleu 1¼ hrs., back to Arolla 1½ hrs.; total time about 5½ hrs.
**Difference in height:** 900m.
**Highest point:** about 2830m.
**Grade:** marked paths, a short, exposed section is made safe with a chain.
**Food and accommodation:** Cabane des Aiguilles Rouges (drinks and usually simple food as well from July to September; tel: 027/2831649).
**Worth seeing:** in the area around Arolla marvellous stands of Swiss pines (hence the name, from the French 'arolle' for stone pine or Swiss pine). View of Mt. Collon, Pigne d'Arolla and the Aiguilles of Arolla. The Lac Bleu does justice to its name and lies like a 'blue eye' in a light stand of Swiss pines and larch trees.

If you plan to stay overnight in the hut you should definitely telephone beforehand. In settled weather do not go back down too early as the surrounding massifs display themselves in their best light during the course of the afternoon.
From **Arolla** follow the road which goes up westwards to the blocks of apartments. At the end of the tarmac road (which continues to Pra Gra as a track) and above the ski lift station turn off at the next bend (unclear signpost) and go uphill through a marvellous pine forest to the upper mountain pastures. With increasingly more waymarkers the path now leads up to

the highest huts of the **Pra Gra alp** where there's a particularly wide panorama. Then, along an old water channel, the path crosses over into the scree basin of Les Ignes. It traverses the run-off from the Ignes glacier opposite the steep morainal flank below the Aiguilles Rouges glacier until it finally leads across a short scree slope to the nearby **Cabane des Aiguilles Rouges**.

Descent to the Lac Bleu: from the hut go about another 200m to the north leisurely uphill until the path winds down the grassy slopes of Les Crosayes to the Louché pastures with the wonderful **Lac Bleu** (a good overview from the hut). South of the lake the path branches off into the rift valley trough of the glacial run-offs which you cross over on a bridge. With some ups-and-downs you walk through the Arolla valley to the south towards Arolla; where the path ascends back up to the huts of Pra Gra, you can return along the lower path through the Swiss pine wood again to **Arolla**. Alternative: direct descent from the Lac Bleu in 20 mins. to La Gouille.

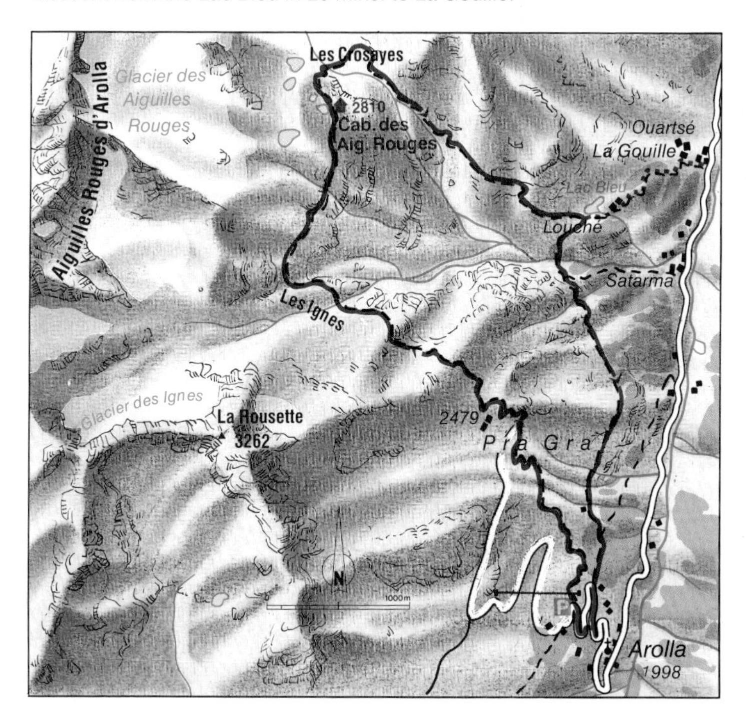

# 22 Plans de Bertol

The furthest corner in the Arolla valley

## Arolla – water container at the Arolla glacier – Plans de Bertol

**Location and starting point:** Arolla, 1998m; for more information see Walk 21.
**Walking times:** Arolla – water container 40 mins., ascent 1¾ hrs.; return 1½ hrs.; total time 3¼ hrs.
**Difference in height:** 700m.
**Highest point:** Plans de Bertol, about 2700m.
**Grade:** easy walk on marked path sometimes over steep ground. No facilities on the way.
**Worth seeing:** wild sérac ledges of the Collon glacier directly opposite the small plateau. The north wall of Mont Collon is justifiably one of the showpieces of the mountains around Arolla.
**NB:** the Plans de Bertol mark about one half of the ascent to the Bertol hut; it's the steep glacier field below the Col de Bertol more than the length of the path and variation in height which challenges an experienced and appropriately equipped mountaineer on the hut ascent. On the other hand, the viewing balcony Plans de Bertol is accessible to every mountain hiker.

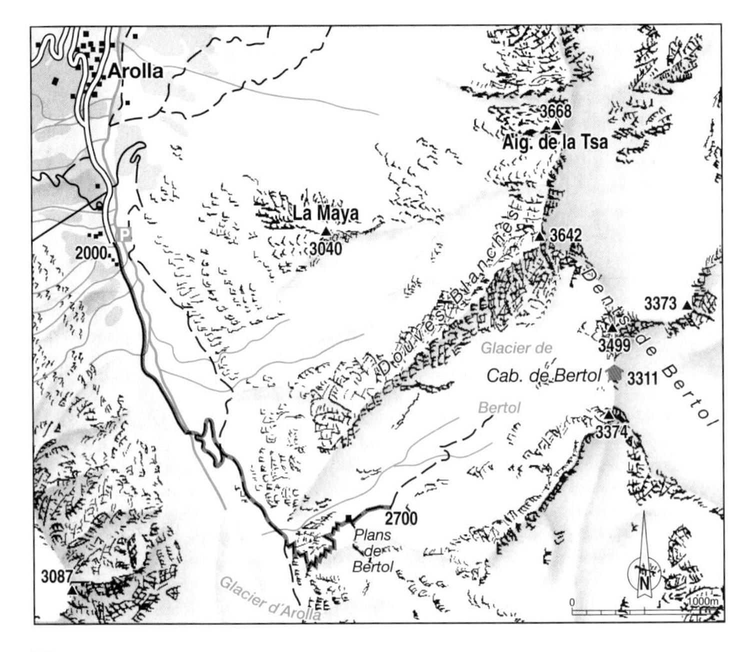

*Mont Collon towers up into the sky, dominating the end of the Arolla valley.*

From the car park at the south end of **Arolla** go along the roadway closed to cars for about 2km into the valley to the end at the bridge near the glacial tongue (signpost). The path goes up the eastern glacier bank south-eastwards, then crosses the run-off from the Bertol glacier and comes to the ruins of the **water tank construction**. At the fork there, the ascent path branches off right to the summits round the Arolla glacier while the path you will take winds steeply up eastwards to the sparsely vegetated plateau of **Plans de Bertol**.
Even if you do not reach a summit there is still a great view, especially of Pigne d'Arolla, Mont Collon and the glacial crevice in between (this view is not significantly better from the 600m higher Bertol hut). However it's worth going a few metres southwards, fairly on the level, to be able to get a complete view of the upper Arolla glacier as well with the surrounding peaks.
The return path goes back the way you came up.

# 23 Mont Blava, 2932m

High above Lac des Dix

## Le Chargeur – Lac des Dix – Cabane de Prafleuri – Col des Roux – Mont Blava – La Barma alp – Lac des Dix

**Location:** Hérémence, 1237m; small village situated high up and with beautiful views above the turn-off to Val d'Hérémence from the Val d' Héréns; wonderful village centre with very postmodern church; good post bus service from Sion.
**Starting point:** Le Chargeur, 2141m, at the foot of the dam of Lac des Dix. Hotel, restaurant and cable car at the top of the dam. Post bus from Sion via Hérémence (4 buses a day, a good hour's journey, 30km). Parking places.
**Walking times:** dam – Cabane de Prafleuri 1¼ hr., hut – Col de Roux ¾ hrs., summit ascent ½ hr., descent via La Barma to the dam 1¼ hrs.; total time just under 4 hrs.
**Difference in height:** 790m.
**Grade:** marked path to the hut and over the pass, sometimes through boulder fields; tracks to the summit where surefootedness is essential.
**Food and accommodation:** Cabane de Prafleuri, 2662m; privately owned, always open, occasionally staffed in summer (enquire in La Chargeur, tel. no. of the hut: 027/2811156). La Barma alp, 2575m; basic food in the season.
**Worth seeing:** the true scale of Lac des Dix from Mont Blava is visible, together with the highest dam in Europe. The biggest part of the building material was transported from the gravel pit of Prafleuri by cable car to the dam (informative exhibition at the power station building in Le Chargeur).

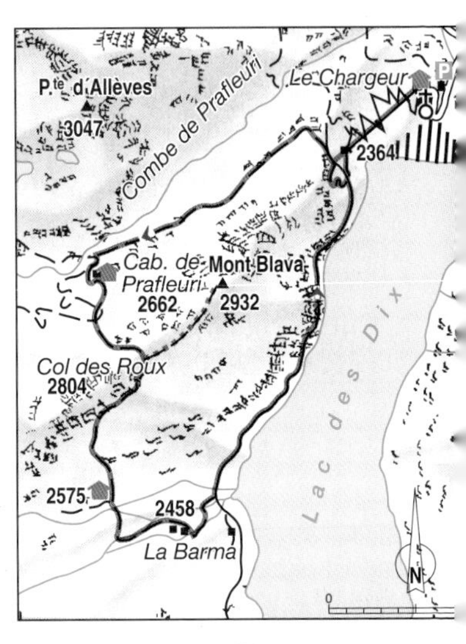


It's convenient to take the cable car from the building of the Dixence company in **Le Chargeur** to the top of the **Lac des Dix** dam, otherwise ascend the footpath in about 45 mins. After a few metres along the bank the broad path bears right and winds up to a ridge where you can already see the **Cabane de Prafleuri** at the back of the valley. The path sometimes goes over boulder fields across the Blava flank, finally passing below the hut which you come to from behind (hikers accustomed to the mountains can take a beautiful shortcut on this last section along some tracks across partly overgrown glacially striated slabs). This basin-shaped valley contains mostly moraine scree, constantly supplied by the glacier with only the traces of the dambuil-

*The end of the Dixence valley with the dam; Mont Blava on the right above.*

ding still recognisable.
Along the path from the hut you quickly reach the **Col des Roux** – the reservoir, as if from another world, now lies at your feet, surrounded by precipitous rocks and shining mountains covered in névé. If you are a sure-footed hiker you should definitely make a detour onto **Mont Blava**: go round a short rock step on the south-facing flank, then keep on the ridge up to the highest point where the panorama is worth the effort. But if you are happy to have reached the notch, you will also be inspired by this view.
Descend from the col to the south, at first over scree slopes, then across the sloping meadows to the **La Barma alp**; as you sit down for a rest you can see opposite the sheer rock peaks of the Aiguilles Rouges. The black and brown Eringer cows graze on the alpine meadows in the foreground. The cows are an old Valaisan species, suited to the mountains, but not conforming to EU regulations in respect of their milk production; they would presumably have already disappeared if they hadn't been the stars of the cow fighting with their notable fighting spirit. This is a Valaisan attraction and in contrast to the Spanish tradition, there's no blood, so it's not even necessary for animal rights protectors to have a guilty conscience when they visit these local festivals. It's a quick descent to the **Lac des Dix** and then there's a final 2km walk on the level back to the dam.

# 24 Cabane des Dix, 2928m

From the enormous reservoir into arctic fields

## Le Chargeur – Lac des Dix – Cabane des Dix – Le Chargeur

**Location:** Hérémence, 1237m; small village situated high up and with beautiful views above the turn-off to Val d'Hérémence from the Val d' Hérens; wonderful village centre with very modern church; good post bus service from Sion.
**Starting point:** Le Chargeur, 2141m, at the foot of the dam of Lac des Dix. Hotel, restaurant and cable car to the top of the dam. Post bus from Sion via Hérémence (4 buses, 1 hr. journey, 30km). Parking places.
**Walking times:** dam – south end of Lac des Dix (a good 7km) 1½ hrs., Ascent to the Cabane des Dix 2 hrs.; return to the lake 1¼ hrs., onward path to the dam 1½ hrs.; total time about 6½ hrs.
**Difference in height:** 790m.
**Grade:** roadway by the lake, then a good hiking path to the hut.
**Food and accommodation:** Cabane des Dix (SAC), staffed from about the beginning of July to the end of Sept. One of the big SAC huts (150 beds), generally well used. For overnight accommodation you need to register with the guardian, tel: 027/2811523.
**Worth seeing:** The dam of Dixence is impressively large. The wall consists of almost 6 million cubic metres of concrete and filling material and it dams up to 400 million cubic metres of water for the production of about 1600 million kilowatt hours of electric energy. The water is channelled from an enormous area, the tunnel system reaches right into the heart of the region around Zermatt. Free guided tour round the dam works in summer. There's a magnificent view onto the north face of Mont Blanc de Cheilon.

The Cabane des Dix is surrounded on three sides by glaciers which give a truly arctic feel to the landscape. No-one should be seduced into going across these glaciers without suitable equipment and experience.
The cable car takes you up the good 200m in altitude from **Le Chargeur** to the top of the dam of **Lac des Dix** (45 mins. on foot). The roadway leads

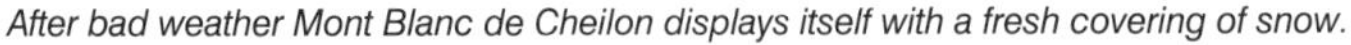

*After bad weather Mont Blanc de Cheilon displays itself with a fresh covering of snow.*

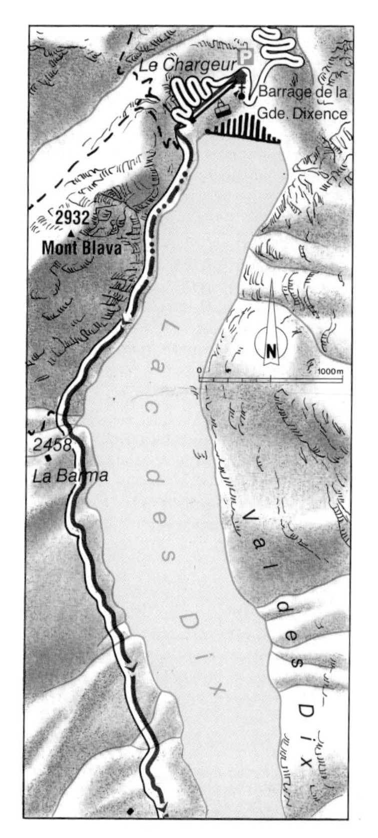


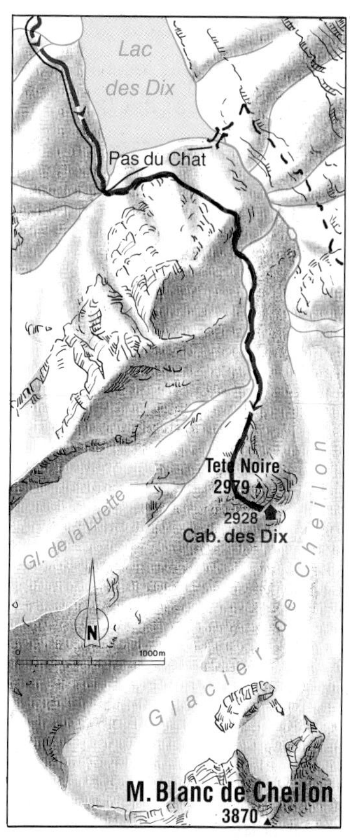


with only a very slight variation in height along the western bank of the lake to the southern end; the slopes of the meadows become a real paradise of flowers here in summer. You turn off from the path which comes from Arolla over the Col de Riedmatten and go up over the slope called 'Pas du Chat' diagonally towards the large glacier basin of the Cheilon glacier. High above its glacial tongue the path now runs along the ridge of the side moraine (which marks the level of the glacier from 100 to 200 years ago – it was, therefore, a good 100m higher than now). The views become increasingly impressive as the path goes around below the Tête Noire crag and then there's a short ascent up to the **Cabane des Dix**. Descend on the same path.

# 25 Croix de la Cha, 2351m

Unusually varied walk with beautiful views above the Rhône valley

**Mosson – Flore alp – Lac d'Etang-de-Trente-Pas – Croix de la Cha**

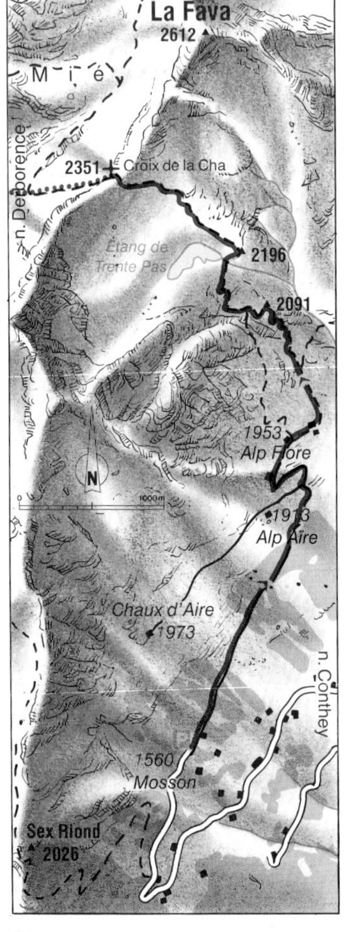


**Location:** Conthey, 511m; small village not far away from Sion below extensive vineyards on the western Bernese Alps. Good bus service to Sion.

**Starting point:** Mosson, 1560m; end of the little tarmac road from Conthey and Erde via Daillon and Mayens de Conthey. Bus service as far as Mayens de Conthey. Parking places in Mosson and, if you're planning the round walk to Derborence, in Sion or Erde.

**Walking times:** Mosson – Flore alp 1½ hrs., Flore – Lac d'Etang-de-Trente-Pas 1 hr., to the col ½ hr.; descent 2 hrs.; total time 5 hrs.

**Difference in height:** 790m.

**Grade:** easy walk on good paths. No facilities on the way.

**Worth seeing:** a drive through the extensive vineyards in the lower area; wonderful view back from the Flore alp into the furrow of the Rhône valley, into Val d'Herens and of all the large peaks of the Valais. Lac d'Etang-de-Trente-Pas lies below the pass. From the pass itself there's a great view of the Diablerets group of mountains.

**NB:** an interesting alternative is to descend from the pass westwards into the Lizerne valley to Derborence, 2 hrs.; return by bus to Erde (2 buses a day in summer).

*The peaks round the Croix de la Cha are formed from vertically towering ancient limestone reefs.*

This walk goes through a classically beautiful high mountain landscape, across pastures and alpine meadows, fields of limestone and cirques full of detritus. At almost every point you are afforded a splendid view of the mountains south of the Rhône valley and the peaks of the Bernese Alps.

A farm track which diagonally crosses the slope, leads from **Mosson** partly through forest and then over open ground – there's an abundance of flowers on either side – to the 1848m point and above to the left up to the Aïre alpe, 1913m. From here go northwards to the **Flore alp**, 1953m. Still going north on a gentle incline head towards a steep section and wind uphill to the 2091m point (interesting deeply grooved terrain on the left). Continue across more level ground to the **Lac d'Etang-de-Trente-Pas**, 2196m and then north-eastwards up to the **Croix de la Cha**.

Go back down the ascent path.

# 26 Derborence – Anzeindaz

A hidden jewel: the youngest naturally formed lake in Switzerland

## Derborence – Pas de Cheville – Anzeindaz

**Location:** Conthey, 511m; neighbouring community of Sion with good bus connections. Erde, 802m; small village above the vineyards of Conthey at the turn-off to the Sanetsch pass.
**Starting point:** Derborence, 1513m; on the lake of the same name, conservation area. PTT bus service from Sion via Erde (2 buses a day, about 1¼ hour's journey, 32km). Audaciously planned, narrow approach road. Parking 300m before the lake.
**Walking times:** Derborence – Pas de Cheville 1½ hrs., onward path to Anzeindaz ½ hr., return about 2 hrs.; total time 4 hrs.
**Difference in height:** 530m.
**Grade:** not a difficult mountain walk on good, marked paths.
**Food and accommodation:** Anzeindaz, 1876m; two huts as well as guest house in Derborence, staffed May to October, accommodation too.
**Worth seeing:** the Lac de Derborence was created by two landslides from the Diablerets in the 18th century. As you go across the expanse of rubble from the approach road you get a close look at the original vegetation in this arid location. The lake displays areas of sedimentation, it is very flat and changes size according to the amount of precipitation. In the steep adjoining forest in the south are to be found examples of gigantic silver firs (over 40m tall, the largest in Switzerland); even though there have been raging storms here in previous years, it's definitely worth taking a short walk round the lake (conservation area).

As you drive to the starting point of this quite short walk which takes you over the canton boundary into the Waadtland, you are able to marvel at the daring road with its many tunnels and galleries through the exceptionally steep rock face and be amazed at one of the highest slabs in the Alps opposite.
The Lac de Derborence with the restaurant is situated only a few minutes from the car park and the bus stop in **Derborence**.

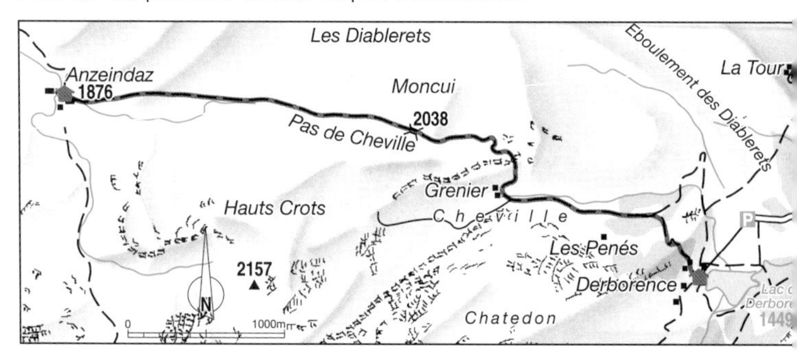

*From the plateau of Pas de Cheville you can see as far as the Valais Alps.*

Just behind, the path winds up a short way into the thin wood and then soon turns off into the Cheville valley. Cross the stream at the Grenier huts and the path ascends round some hairpin bends through a gully flanked on both sides with rock precipices to the plateau above. You soon reach the **Pas de Cheville** where the wild southern precipices of the Diablerets are particularly imposing, and thankfully, you can see nothing of the summer skiing area on its northern side. The snowy peaks of the Valais Alps are visible across the Lizerne gorge, the Weisshorn in front of them all.
Almost due west the path brings you gently downhill into the **Anzeindaz** basin where you will be sure to find a place to eat, and also accommodation for the night.
Go back along the same route.

# 27 L'Ardevaz (L'Ardève), 1501m

Bold ridge with views high above the Rhône valley

**Ovronnaz / Mayens de Chamoson – L'Ardevaz**

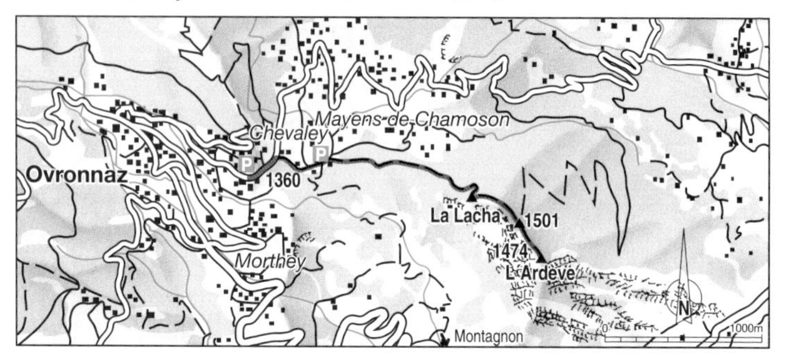


**Locations:** Leytron, 501m, and Chamoson, 610m; wine villages in the lower Rhône valley on characteristic alluvial cones, bus service to Sion.
**Starting point:** Ovronnaz, Chevaley hamlet, 1360m; post bus stop (about 9 buses a day from Leytron, journey of 30 mins., 13km); by car to Mayens de Chamoson, turn-off from the link road to Ovronnaz at a junction a little way before the col (1310m, signpost, parking).
**Walking times:** just under 1 hr. to the summit (1¼ hrs. from Ovronnaz), ¾ hrs. return; total time 1¾ hrs.
**Difference in height:** 140m.
**Grade:** even if this is a very short walk it demands absolute sure-footedness and a lack of vertigo as it goes along a precipice and in places is also very steep; with a short secured section in between. Under no circumstances do this walk after it has rained as the path becomes very slippery and dangerous. No facilities on the way.
**Worth seeing:** there are not many places in the Alps where you can stand so high and so vertically above a bustling valley – 1000m above the vineyards which are at the foot of these chaotic rock faces. Mont Blanc, Grand Combin and Bietschhorn are some of the prominent landmarks which can be seen in the distance.

The wedge-shaped face of Ardevaz catches your eye on the drive from Martigny up the Rhône; the mountain is part of the 'Morcles blanket' from an enormous fold where one part is layered in the normal way and another is in reverse, causing older rock to be lying on top of younger rock.
From **Ovronnaz-Chevaley** continue about 200m along the road, then on a narrow path to the right down to the lowest point at the start of the Ardevaz ridge (parking places here too). It's a leisurely walk in the shade along the ridge itself, and then just before 'La Lacha' rock it gets very steep – to the right you can already enjoy the first breathtakingly beautiful views down the

mountain. Go round the left-hand side of the following rocks up a steep earthy path after a short scrambling section. Soon after that you come back to the top of the ridge. Now, keeping to the ridge or a little to the left below it, continue to the highest point of **L'Ardevaz**; but it's not till further on that you have the best view at the 1474m point where the mountain breaks off down steep rock faces to the south and west and allows you a totally open view.
Return on the same path, but be careful on the descent over a steep section close to the ridge.

*Looking back from the ascent of Ardevaz into the Ovronnaz basin.*

# 28 Grand Garde, 2145m

Beautiful high mountain walk to a mountain with sheer rock faces dropping down into the Rhône valley and stunning views

## Ovronnaz – Petit Pré – Grand Garde – Tête du Betson – Ovronnaz

**Location:** Ovronnaz, 1420m; holiday village situated high above the Rhône valley. Buses to Leytron (about 9 a day, journey of 30 mins., 13km).
**Starting point:** Ordonne, 1597m; alpine pasture a little above Ovronnaz which you can drive to on a narrow roadway.
**Walking times:** Ordonne – Petit Pré 1¼ hrs., ridge path to Grand Garde ¾ hrs., descent to the Tête du Betson ¾ hrs., return to Ordonne ½ hr.; total time 3¼ hrs.
**Difference in height:** 550m.
**Grade:** easy walk on good marked paths, some rough forest paths in places. No places to eat on the way.
**Worth seeing:** as with all the walks in the area of Muveran-Diablerets you can study some wonderful rock strata: the top layers of 'Helvetian blankets', with some gigantic folds in places, are the sedimentary deposits of the ancient lake (Tethis) dating from the origin of the Alps, and so revealing a preponderance of limestone with intermediary layers of clay and marl.

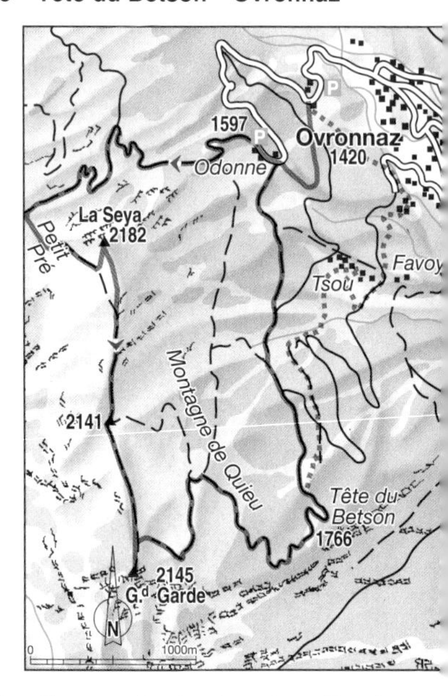


Grand Garde, the 'great guardian', offers on its back – just like its neighbours – a very hiker-friendly mountain ridge with a sheer drop down to the Rhône valley. The high location of Ovronnaz keeps the demands of the ascent within very tolerable limits.

Start the walk at the **Ordonne alp** which you can reach either by car along a narrow road from the sports centre or along a footpath in a good 30 mins. From here walk leisurely along the track into the next valley cleft, branch off left there and go uphill to the Petit Pré alp. This alpine meadow lies at the start of the Euloi plateau in the basin-shaped valley below Dent Favre, Muveran and Chavalard. The onward path bears sharply to the left up to the Montagne de Quieu mountain ridge. You reach the ridge after a short ascent near to **La Seya** hill, where it's worth taking a short detour, before walking along the ridge to **Grand Garde** with a marvellous panorama all the way. The

*At the La Seya viewpoint: Haut de Cry above the Ovronnaz basin.*

ridge breaks off here with a frighteningly steep and loose rock face down to the Rhône valley, a genuine 'highpoint' of the walk for panoramic views and views down into the valley.
On the descent turn to the left and go eastwards downhill along a path through a thin stand of larch trees to an alpine meadow where you meet an alpine path taking you further down the valley to the edge of the precipice again above the Rhône valley at **Tête du Betson** (end of a track from Ovronnaz). Follow the track downhill as far as the third bend where a good path leads across the flank back to **Ordonne**.
If you would prefer to descend to **Ovronnaz**, take a shortcut from the track a little below Tête du Betson along the old footpath to Tsou and from here go across to the sports centre or straight over to the village.

# 29 Lac de Fully

Blue-green lakes like eyes and a viewing balcony par excellence

**L'Erié – Lac de Fully – Cabane du Demècre – Tête du Portail – L'Erié**

**Location:** Fully, 473m, extensive wine and fruit growing community at the elbow of the Rhône, only 5km away from Martigny. Buses to Martigny.
**Starting point:** small alpine meadows at L'Erié, 1850m, along an excitingly steep, but little tarmac road from Fully via the small hamlets of Eulo, Buitonne and Chibo, then on a gravel alpine meadow path across the Randonne rift valley; small car park.
**Walking times:** L'Erié – Lac de Fully. 1½ hrs., ascent to the Cabane du Demècre ¾ hrs., onward path to Tête du Portail ¾ hrs., return to L'Erié 1¼ hrs.; total time 4 – 4½ hrs.
**Difference in height:** 620m.
**Highest point:** Le Diabley, 2469m.
**Grade:** good, adequately marked hiking paths, but a confident lack of vertigo is essential as you cross steep slopes.
**Food and accommodation:** Cabane de Sorgno on Lac de Fully, 2064m, tel: 027/7462426; Cabane du Demècre on the col of the same name, 2361m, tel: 027/7461019; simple food is provided only in summer, but at other times of year the huts are still open; possible overnight accommodation.
**Worth seeing:** there are seldom panoramic paths so high and so steep above the valley floor; the lower lake has a natural origin, the upper one has been dammed; together with the fabulous views of the Valais from the Cabane du Demècre there are also magnificent views of the Dents du Midi and towards the Mont Blanc group.

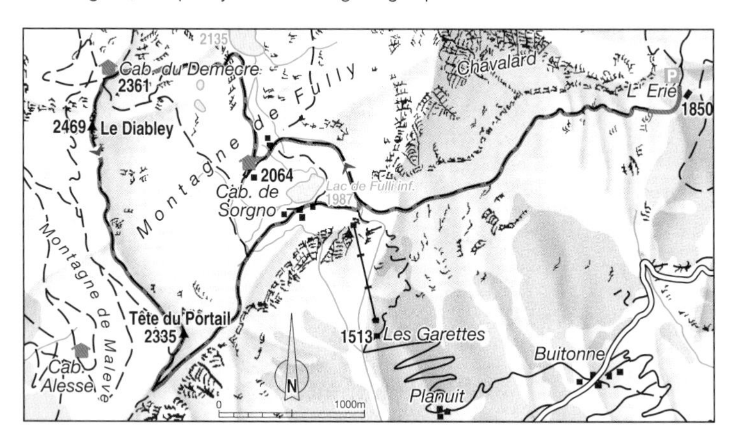


After the courageous drive up the steep little road from Fully there's not much time to recover at the car park of the L'Erié alp, before taking the path onto the steep flank below Chavalard.

*Excitingly airy viewpoint at the Tête du Portail you can enjoy the views high above the Rhône valley.*

Follow here a large overgrown strip between sheer rock cliffs and after that up a gentle incline, you come to the edge at the Fully basin. The path curves round the lower **Lac de Fully** to the Cabane de Sorgno – this first stop for refreshments is highly recommended.
The onward path leads up the valley over a small ledge to the dam of the upper Lac de Fully; turn off left (west) and go uphill across the grassy terrain interspersed with smooth rocks. You soon come to the Col de Demècre with the **Cabane du Demècre** almost hidden in a furrow – it's hard not to stop for refreshments here too (but please do not forget to pay if the warden is not there – both huts are extremely well equipped for self-catering, and it should be kept that way).
Briefly, but steeply the path then goes up to Le Diabley and from there follows the ridge in a southerly direction with excellent views as far as the **Tête du Portail**, the most south-westerly point of the Bernese Alps – an ideal resting place here on the summit on a warm summer's afternoon, studying the Dents du Midi, Mont Blanc and Grand Combin with binoculars or watching the bustling activities of Martigny way down below in the bottom of the valley.
The last stage of the walk now goes to the east, breathtakingly high above the valley, back down to the lower Lac de Fully, where after a few paces, you come back to the first part of the ascent from **L'Erie**.

# 30 Dent de Nendaz, 2463m – Balavaux larch trees

From the edge of a skiing area to the tallest larch trees in Switzerland

**Tracouet – Dent de Nendaz – Balavaux alp – Tracouet**

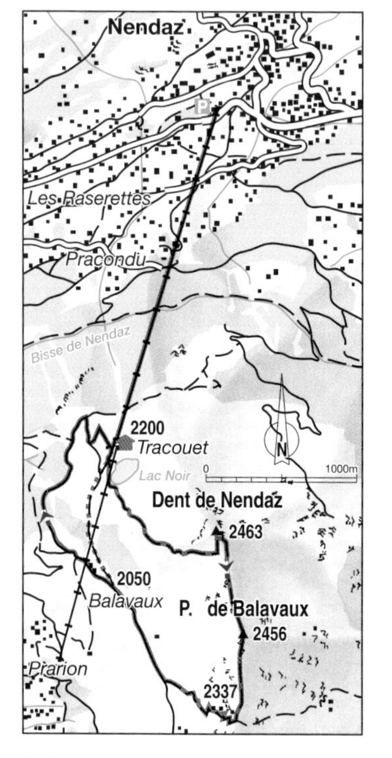


**Location:** Haute Nendaz, 1365m; post bus to Sion (frequent buses, about 22km).

**Starting point:** Station Tracouet, 2200m; cable railway from Haute Nendaz, open in summer from about 8.30 until 17.00. About 2 hours on foot along good paths in the forest and across ski slopes. From the Nendaz – Isérables road an unpaved, narrow and steep track branches off to the alpine holiday settlement of Prarion and further on to Balavaux alp.

**Walking times:** Tracouet – Dent de Nendaz ¾ hrs, to the Pointe de Balavaux ½ hr., descent to the Balavaux Alpe ¾ hrs., to Tracouet 40 mins.; total time a good 2½ hrs.

**Difference in height:** 270m.

**Grade:** easy mountain walk on good paths.

**Food and accommodation:** in Tracouet station.

**Worth seeing:** the larch trees of Balavaux are absolutely unique – trees with trunks of such a large diameter that are hardly found anywhere else in the Alps – the well-known picturesque stature of these enormous trees at the tree line is in itself worth a visit to this high mountain park. Some trees have a diameter of over 2 metres and a proven age of over 1000 years.

A few paces from **Tracouet station** and you come to Lac Noir, a marshy lake with extremely dark water. The well marked path leads past the lake and up to the west ridge. Either go directly up the ridge covered with boulders or just below it on the south side to the nearby **Dent de Nendaz** – you've hardly got warmed up before you reach the top. By the way: a tunnel leads from Lac des Dix up to just below the summit and then goes down into the Rhône valley as a pressure pipe – and so a doubling of energy output has been achieved (compare Walk 23). Now walk southwards along the ridge without any problems to the next rise, Pointe de Balavaux; from here

there's not much left to see of the nearby skiing area, and the view is still outstanding.
A short descent leads southwards to the next notch where two paths cross: left goes into the Nendaz valley, straight on goes up over the ridge to the Plan du Fou – therefore into the ski lift area of Super Nendaz. However, you descend the path to the right westwards, to **Balavaux alp**. Round some hairpin bends you reach the area of the forestry boundary where you find yourself standing under the enormous larch trees. There are some superb examples to be found just below the track which you will take to walk back to the starting point.
From the mountain pasture you can take a shortcut along a firebreak to **Tracouet**, but the track can also be thoroughly recommended for the return route due to the beautiful views.

*Looking back to the bend in the river near Martigny from the ascent to Dent de Nendaz.*

# 31 Col des Planches – Pas du Lin, 1656m

Marvellous alpine pastures with fabulous stands of larches

## Martigny – Chemin – Col des Planches – Pas du Lin – Levron – Sembrancher

**Starting point:** Martigny, 476m; junction between the Rhône valley and the Aosta and Chamonix route.
Starting point for the trains to Châtelard / Chamonix (MC railway) and to Orsières / Le Châble (Bernard-Express, MO railway), motorway connection to Lausanne and Sion.
**Destination:** Sembrancher, 717m; at the confluence of the Dranse valleys (Val de Bagnes, Val d'Entremont), station for the Bernard-Express, main road from Martigny to Aosta.
**Walking times:** Martigny – Chemin 2 hrs. (convenient bus too), ascent to the Col des Planches 1 hr., to the Pas du Lin 1 hr., descent to Levron 40 mins.; return to Sembrancher 1½ hrs. (better by bus).; total time 6 hrs.
**Difference in height:** 1180m.
**Grade:** easy walk on good paths.
**Food and accommodation:** guest house in Chemin Dessous (viewing terrace), Chemin (wonderful old hotel building), Col des Planches and Pas du Lin (beautiful alpine pasture with solitary trees and beautiful view), guest houses in Leytron, Vollèges and Sembrancher.
**Worth seeing:** from Chemin Dessous you have the best view of Martigny and the lower Rhône valley, also a beautiful view from Chemin onwards of the Combin mountains with marvellous larch trees in the foreground.

There is a small road running parallel to this route. You cross it several times and actually walk along it over short sections, but the area is very beautiful and there are long sections where you do not come into contact with the road at all.
The ascent to Chemin begins directly behind the cemetery of **Martigny**, accessible from the centre through the old part of the town in the direction of the Expo. It leads steeply up through the wood to Chemin Dessous, a settlement in a clearing with beautiful views and then again through dense wood as it ta-

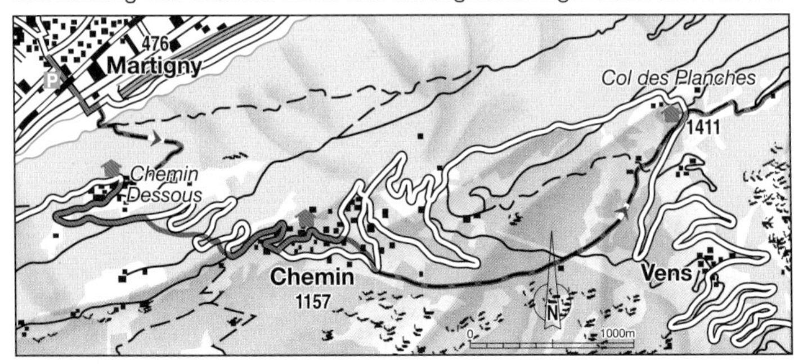

kes a shortcut across the bends in the road. There was a fashionable summer resort here more than 100 years ago, as you can see from the style of many old buildings in **Chemin**. The onward path goes up diagonally across the south side of the ridge with beautiful views down into the Drance valley, crosses a dry wood and reaches the **Col des Planches** alpine pastures.
For the ridge walk to the Pas du Lin it's more convenient to take the roadway which has a gravel surface and on the way you come past the Col du Tronc (turn-off for a shortcut to Levron as well as for the detour to La Crevasse viewpoint which affords you an open view of the whole area; about a 40 minute ascent and then 20 minutes back down to the Col du Tronc) followed by a walk through a particularly beautiful stand of larch trees to the **Pas du Lin**.
For the descent to Levron branch off right from the road, descend a bit further below a rocky area and then you soon arrive at the village. We recommend that you take the bus from here to Sembrancher, otherwise descend along the path across the meadows till you reach the overgrown alluvial cone at Cries, washed down from the basin-shaped valley below Pierre Avoi, and then continue directly to Vollèges. The last section goes partly along the road and partly on meadow paths down to **Sembrancher**.

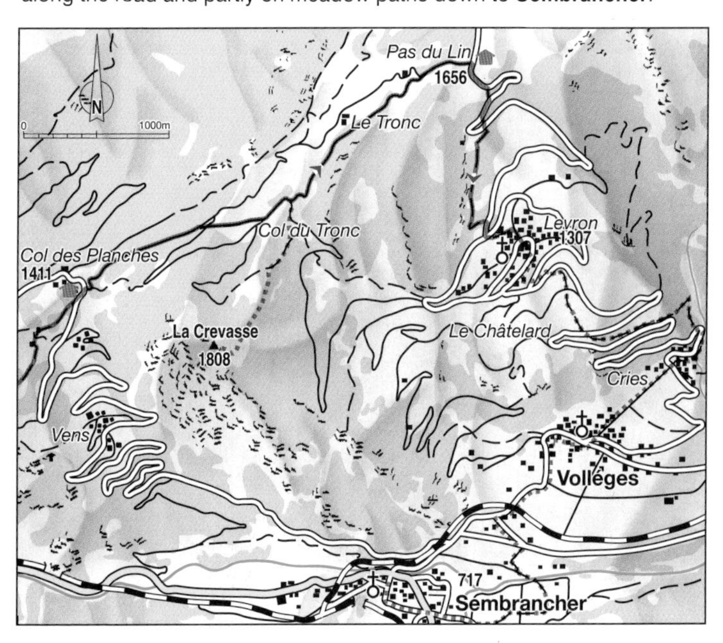

# 32 Pierre Avoi, 2473m

Viewing high point above the Rhône elbow in the Rhône near Martigny

## Savoleyres – Pierre Avoi – Mayens de Riddes

**Location:** Mayens de Riddes (Tzoumaz), 1520m. Riddes, 475m, SBB/CFF-stop; from there buses to Mayens de Riddes (3 buses a day, 25 – 30 mins. journey) or bus to Isérables (5 a day), which is linked to Riddes by cable car (in operation between about 6.00 and 20.30).
**Starting point:** mountain station of the cable railway Mayens de Riddes – Savoleyres, 2354m (open end of June – beginning Sept.). Parking at the valley station.
**Walking times:** Savoleyres – Pierre Avoi 50 mins., return to Mayens de Riddes 2¼ hrs.; total time a good 3 hrs.
**Difference in height:** 120m up, 800m down.
**Grade:** very good hiking paths up to about 30m below the summit where there's a steep section leading up to the top, made easy with steps and handrails.
**Food and accommodation:** Savoleyres mountain station and restaurant at Les Etablons.
**Worth seeing:** in spite of the considerable intrusions into nature (alpine roads and lifts) you will find meadows here ablaze with flowers and on the high ledge below, the most beautiful larch wood (the ski circus of 'Quatre Vallées' is adjacent to this walking area to the south-east). On the drive up beautiful view of the western Bernese Alps and far down into the Rhône valley and from the mountain station, a great view of the Combin and Mont Blanc ranges.

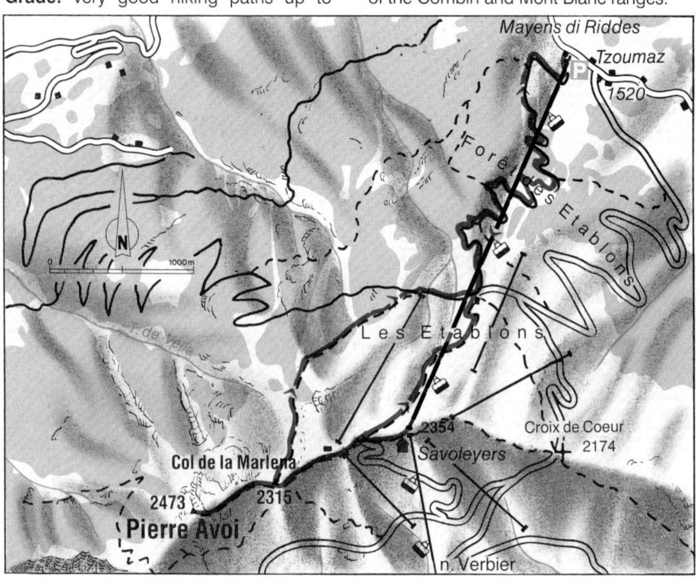

*The rock tooth of Pierre Avoi towers high above the Rhône valley.*

The roadway to the Croix de Coeur and to Savoleyres is in very bad condition and part of your mountain experience would literally fall by the wayside. In any case, you would miss out on the really beautiful descent from Savoleyres to Mayens de Riddes. Savoleyres can also be reached by cable railway from Verbier.
From the mountain station in **Savoleyres** the good path goes unerringly along the broad ridge (you can quite happily follow the uppermost paths and the view is worth it) onto the south-east side of the rocky summit area. The short final climb to the **Pierre Avoi** is safely and easily accomplished in a few minutes by a via ferrata, steps cut into the rock and a cable handrail for anyone who has a touch of vertigo.
Return to Mayens de Riddes: from the summit turn back as far as the notch called 'Col de la Marlena', 2315 m, signpost. Follow the good path here to Les Etablons, passing through a wonderful light stand of larch trees. The rest of the twisting descent to **Mayens de Riddes** follows the rough forest path in the area of the forest clearing of the cable railway.

# 33 Sentier des Chamois

Perfect view of the Grand Combin, high above the Val de Bagnes

**Verbier – Les Ruinettes – Cabane du Mont Fort – Col Termin – Lac de Louvie – Fionnay**

**Starting point:** Verbier, about 1500m; post bus and cable car with frequent service from Le Châble (terminus of the Bernard-Express from Martigny, turn-off into Val de Bagnes). Best to park in Le Châble, since this is the point you return to after the walk.
**Destination:** Fionnay, 1490m; post bus to Le Châble (4 buses a day, enquire about the last bus before you start the walk, about 17.30).
**Walking times:** Verbier – Les Ruinettes by cable car (2 hrs. on foot), Les Ruinettes – Cabane du Mont Fort 1 hr., Sentier des Chamois to the Col Termin 1½ hrs., descent to the Lac de Louvie ½ hr., to Fionnay 1 hr.; total time 4 or 6 hrs.
**Difference in height:** 550m.
**Highest point:** Col Termin, 2648m.
**Grade:** good, marked paths, but across very steep flanks in places, so a lack of vertigo is essential.
**Food and accommodation:** Cabane du Mont Fort, SAC, and Refuge du Bouquetin, on Lac de Louvie, private; both establishments are staffed in summer and also offer overnight accommodation.
**Worth seeing:** the whole length of the path is a viewing promenade opposite the Grand Combin; mountain goats are called 'Chamois', but you're more likely to come across ibex (Bouquetin) which are often found here. Be careful: it's not unheard of for these animals to send loose stones down the steep slopes which accumulate high speed and arrive without a sound because of the grassy vegetation – so, especially on the last section before the Col Termin, do not hang around in the gullies and keep an eye on the ground above, particularly if there are animals about.
**Alternative:** a water channel starts in the basin-shaped valley below the Cabane du Mont Fort. It was constructed in the early middle ages and carried the water northwards above Verbier and through the chaotic rock basin below Pierre Avoi as far Levron (Bisse du Levron). It has been restored in places and provides an interesting walk too.

*Left: the panorama of the Combin is a constant companion along the mountain path.*
*Below: the 'mountain goat path' runs through a colony of ibex.*

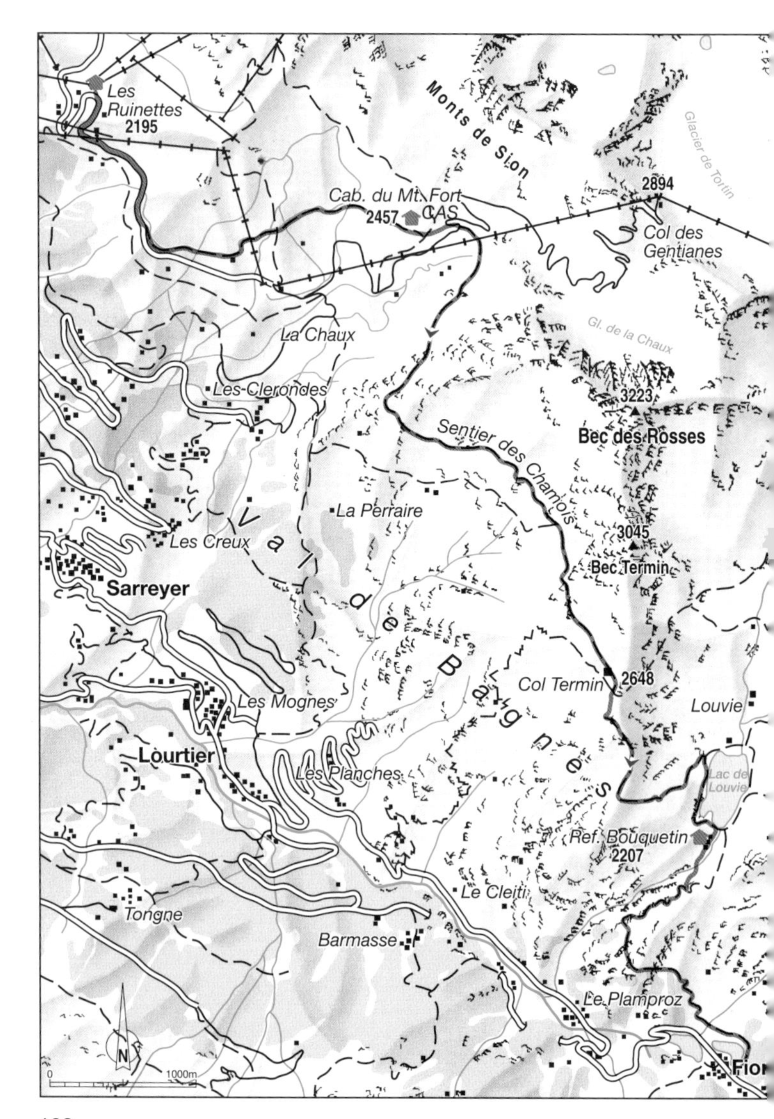
Les Ruinettes
2195
Monts de Sion
Glacier de Tortin
2894
Cab. du Mt. Fort CAS
2457
Col des Gentianes
La Chaux
Gl. de la Chaux
Les-Clerondes
3223
Bec des Rosses
Sentier des Chamois
La Perraire
Val de Bagnes
Les Creux
3045
Bec Termin
Sarreyer
Col Termin
2648
Louvie
Les Mognes
Lourtier
Les Planches
Lac de Louvie
Ref. Bouquetin
2207
Le Cleiti
Tongne
Barmasse
Le Plamproz
N
0
1000m

*View of the Combin at dusk in the vicinity of the Cabane du Mont Font.*

From **Les Ruinettes** station go across the area of ski slopes almost on the level along the broad roadway, where the last short section up to the **Cabane du Mont Fort** gets steeper. You have to descend just under 10m in altitude from the hut into the uppermost basin of the La Chaux alpine meadows, then the **Sentier des Chamois** goes uphill to a first ridge where a particularly beautiful view opens up of the Grand Combin. Now cross the wide basin below the Bec des Rosses, continuing over small ribs of rock and rift valleys, at least across the steep slope of meadows up to the **Col Termin**. You can reach the hill next to it in a few minutes across steep meadows and loose rocky terrain, with a view down to **Lac de Louvie**. The path now runs westwards below the summit down by the Têtes de Louvie and then swings towards the Lac de Louvie with the Refuge du Bouquetin on its southern shore.
At the rift valley created by the run-off from the lake the descent continues steeply down the valley. As soon as you come across the first trees the path bends to the left across the Val de Bagnes and leads over a flank strewn with rocks to the steep meadows above **Fionnay**, which is then quickly reached round a few hairpin bends.

# 34 Mont Brûlé, 2569m

Station between Val de Bagnes and Val d'Entremont with beautiful views

**Moay / La Côt – Le Larzey alp – Six Blanc – Mont Brûlé – Ecuries de Mille – La Côt or Bruson**

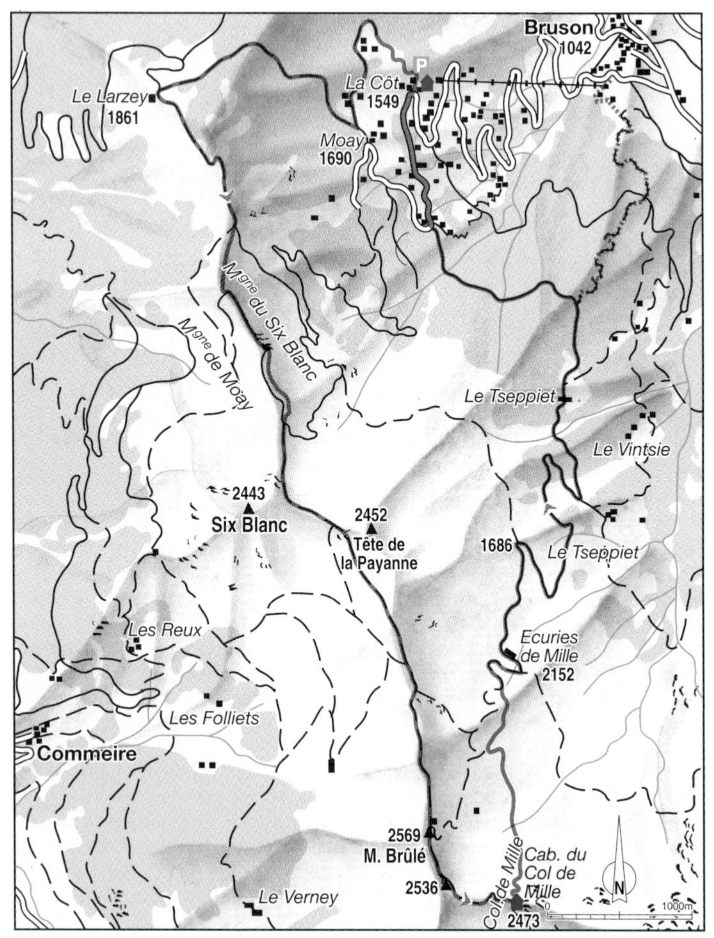

**Location:** Bruson, 1042m; quiet village on a terrace of meadows above Le Châble. Postbus connection from there (up to 8 buses a day, 10 minute journey);
Le Châble is the terminus of the Bernard-Express (MO railway line) from Martigny.
**Starting point:** Moay, 1690m; alpine settlement and small skiing area above Bruson. Post bus service to Le Châble and Bruson (in summer 2 buses a day, 15km, 35 minutes journey).
**Walking times:** Moay / La Côt – Le Larzey 30 mins., ridge walk to Mont Brûlé 2¼ hrs., return via the Cab. du Col de Mille to La Côt (bus) 2 hrs. or directly into Bruson 2½ – 3 hrs.; total time 5 or 6 hrs.
**Difference in height:** 880m.
**Grade:** not a difficult walk (part of the Tour du Val de Bagnes), some short sections of descent along unclear tracks.
**Food and accommodation:** restaurant in La Côt at the bus stop. Cabane du Col de Mille, staffed from the middle of June to the middle of October, tel: 027/ 2211516.
**Worth seeing:** beautiful views into Val d'Entremont and Val de Bagnes as well as of Mont Blanc and the Grand Combin.

*View across Val de Bagnes of Mont Font (the Sentier des Chamois runs along the snow boundary, Walk 33).*

From the bus terminus in **Moay** follow the path to **Le Larzey alp** (signpost; TVB = Tour du Val de Bagnes), a wonderful little place with a thin stand of larch trees high above the valley. Continue along the TVB to a ridge which goes uphill all the way to **Six Blanc**. The TVB branches off to the left here, but your path stays on the ridge and then leaves Six Blanc on the right hand side and crosses directly over to the next summit, the Tête de la Payanne. Go round this to the right to a broad col (Basset). Now go straight along the ridge again or below it on the right to the summit of **Mont Brûlé**.
The descent goes southwards into the Col de Mille with the new hut and then winds down steeply to the north. Gently sloping downhill in the same direction over alpine pastures the path is not really obvious, but you can't miss the **Ecuries de Mille**, an enormous, modern cattle shed. Now descend the long track as far as **La Côt** bus stop or about 500m after the small alpine meadow of Le Tseppiet take the footpath (signpost) directly down to **Bruson** – timewise only a little longer, but it's 600m in altitude of knee-grinding descent.

# 35 Col des Avouillons, 2647m

At the foot of the Petit Combin

**Cabane Brunet – Pron Sery – Col des Avouillons – Corbassière glacier – La Maye – Cabane Brunet**

*Evening light at the Cabane Brunet, dominated by the north flank of the Petit Combin.*

**Location:** Lourtier, 1072m; small village before the ledge of the valley where the Drance de Bagnes narrows below Fionnay. Post bus service to the terminus of the Bernard-Expess in Le Châble (about 10 buses a day, 8km, 15 minute journey).
**Starting point:** Cabane Brunet, 2103m; private mountain hut in a marvellous location at the forest boundary high above Val de Bagnes. Road from Lourtier (taxi or your own car, parking nearby the hut) or about 3 hrs. on foot along a shady, marked forest path.
**Walking times:** Cabane Brunet – Col des Avouillons 2 hrs., return 2 hrs.; total time 4 hrs.
**Difference in height:** 650m.
**Grade:** easy mountain walk on marked paths.
**Food and accommodation:** the Cabane Brunet is staffed all year round and offers good overnight accommodation. It's a good idea to travel there the day before, tel: 077/284916.
**Worth seeing:** it's worth spending a day of your holidays roaming around the vicinity of the hut; the basin-shaped valley below the north face of Petit Combin is particularly worth taking a look at with its many meandering streams in the gravel plain. At the Col des Avouillons there's an imposing view of the Corbassière glacier.

This is not an overly long walk for a day's undertaking, but if you drive up to the hut and back and eat there too, you will find the day rather limited. You should therefore plan to stay overnight at the hut which will also allow you to start the walk at daybreak – an especially delightful experience. There would then be time for a detour across the Corbassieère glacier to the Cabane de Panossière (see Walk 36).
From **Cabane Brunet** wind up along the roadway to the ridge with beautiful views and the alpine hut Ecurie de Sery. The footpath branches off left here

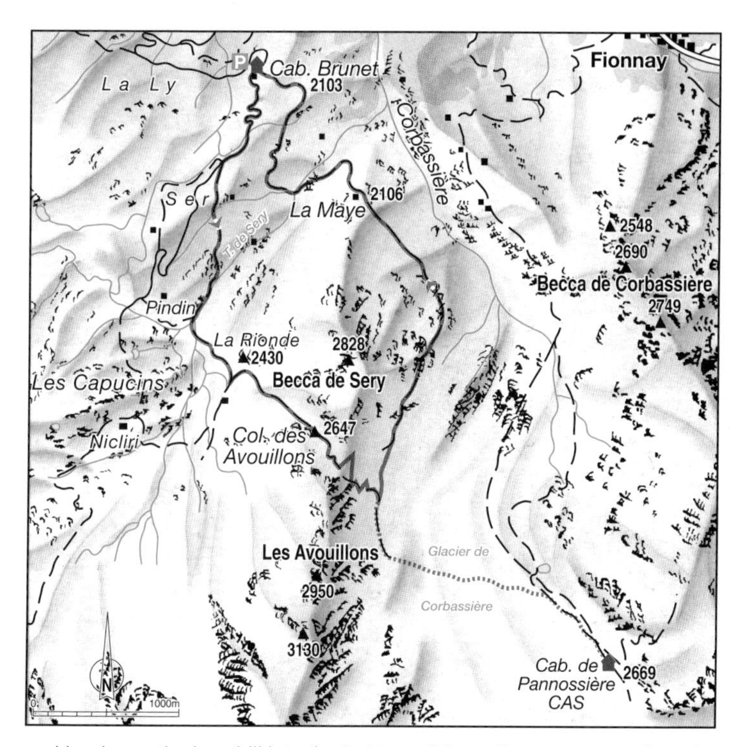


and leads gently downhill into the bottom of the valley, past smooth rocks **Pron Sery**. Go across Sery stream on the bridge and up over alpine pastures on the other side, all the time with wonderful views of the north flank of the Petit Combin. The path finally leads uphill in a small cirque to the **Col des Avouillons** where the view over onto the other side is quite astounding, and of the enormous ice flow of the Corbassière glacier – a marvellous place for a good rest.

Descend hairpin bends down to the side moraine of the **Corbassière glacier** (in good weather you can cross the glacier easily along the pole markings to the Cabane de Panossière, there and back 2 hrs.). The path now goes beside the old moraine down the valley, and round Becca de Sery. At **La Maye alp** you find yourself standing opposite the **Cabane Brunet**, although you are still separated from it by a descent down of nearly 150m in all into the valley bottom with a just as high an ascent up a small narrow path.

# 36 Col des Otanes, 2846m

In the vast arctic world of the Grand Combin

## Mauvoisin – Col des Otanes – Cabane de Panossière – Mauvoisin

**Location:** Fionnay, 1490m; small village in Val de Bagnes.
**Starting point:** Lac de Mauvoisin. With its roughly 250m high dam the reservoir stands only a little way back behind the famous Lac des Dix in the neighbouring valley. Post bus from Fionnay (4 buses a day, a good 15 minute journey, 8km). Parking at the Mauvoisin restaurant on the level area of the 1841m point.
**Walking times:** Mauvoisin – Col des Otanes 4 hrs.; descent to the Cabane de Panossière ¼ hr., return to the pass ½ hr.; descent to Mauvoisin 2½ hrs.; total time about 7 – 8 hrs.
**Difference in height:** 1010m.
**Grade:** alpine walk on a good marked mountain path.
**Food and accommodation:** Restaurant Mauvoisin; as a detour Cabane de Panossière, SAC, 2669m, a modern hut built near the glacier, after the old hut was completely destroyed by an avalanche in 1988.
**Worth seeing:** beautiful views of the reservoir and the glacial mountains rising up behind, such as Mont Blanc de Cheilon; rich flora. From the Col des Otanes there's a perfect view into the Corbassière glacier with the Grand Combin.

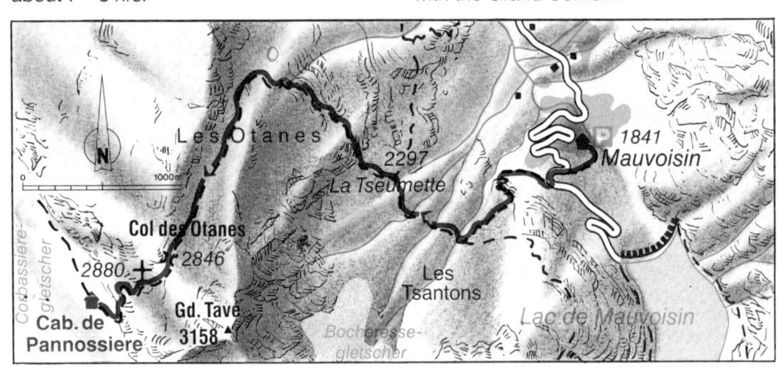


Because of the highly individual architecture of the new Cabane de Panossière (diagonally cut cylinder) the Geneva branch of the SAC has received strong opposition from the valley community.
From Restaurant **Mauvoisin** you go along the power station road as far as the next bend higher up where the path branches off at a signpost in a westerly direction. Zigzag up the steep ledge above on the left which is strewn with rocks; at the top bend there's an especially fine view of the reservoir and down into the valley.
On a moderate incline the path now crosses into the cirque of Les Tsantons and after crossing some streams, leads to Tseumette alp, 2297m, on the far side.

*The ice-covered Grand Combin dominates the huge Corbassière glacier.*

The onward path skilfully winds up through the steep sloping meadows strewn with rocks into the next cirque which leads down from the col. Go over some smooth humps to reach the opposite side where the path then leads in a fairly straight line south-westwards across scree, and possibly old snow fields as well, to the broad col. From the **Col des Otanes** the path crosses the detritus and snow fields below the tiny Otanes glacier to another indistinct col near the 2880m point, where you have the finest view of the Corbassière glacier basin.
Descent to the **Cabane de Panossière**: the good path winds down to the moraine wall where it leads to the right in about 500m to the hut.
The return is back down the ascent path.

# 37 Lac de Mauvoisin – Cabane de Chanrion

Gigantic dam at the foot of the Grand Combin

## Mauvoisin – Lancet – Cabane de Chanrion – Col de Tsofeiret – Mauvoisin

**Location:** Fionnay, 1490m; small village in Val de Bagnes. Bus service from the terminus of the Bernard-Express in Le Châble.
**Starting point:** Lac de Mauvoisin, for more information see Walk 36.
**Walking times:** Mauvoisin – end of the reservoir 1½ hrs., ascent to the Cabane de Chanrion 2 hrs., hut – Col de Tsofeiret 1 hr., return to the reservoir 2 hrs.; total time about 7 hrs.
**Difference in height:** 820m.
**Highest point:** Col de Tsofeiret, about 2630m.
**Grade:** an easy, but really long walk.
**Food and accommodation:** Cabane de Chanrion, 2462m, SAC; staffed from the beginning / middle of July to the middle/ end of September (enquire in the valley), overnight accommodation; tel: 027/ 7781209.
**Worth seeing:** the neighbouring Dix dam is the highest and largest in Europe, but the Mauvoisin dam is certainly the most daring, it is overhanging in the middle like a vault and fans out in the two flanks – it's hard to believe that something like that would hold. After the water level rise in the previous years it is almost as high as the Dixence dam. In high summer the steep grassy slopes on both sides of the lake are ablaze with flowers, and if only for this it's worth taking your time and extending the walk to two days with an overnight stay at the Cabane de Chanrion. From there you can have comprehensive views of the unknown east side of the Grand Combin.

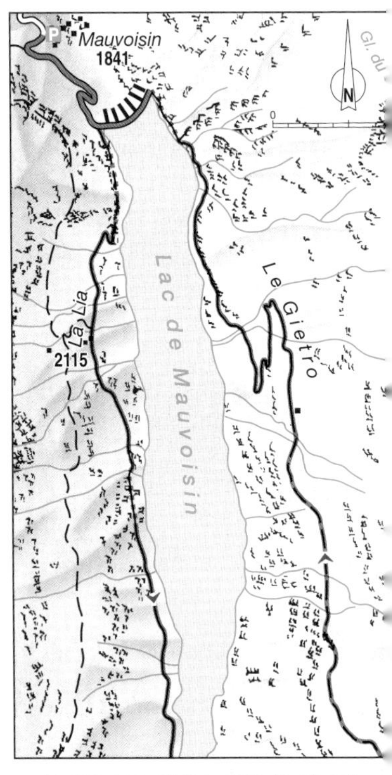


From the **Mauvoisin** car park climb up to the top of the dam in about 15 mins. and then follow the roadway through the good 700m long tunnels along the western bank of the lake. The path goes leisurely uphill to La Lia Alpe and then runs downhill again, excitingly cut through an area of rocks, to the southern end of the reservoir. At Lancet a bridge crosses over the inlet where you can take a shortcut along a narrow path across the following

*The Cabane de Chanrion, dominated by Bec d'Epicoune with its splendid ice ridge.*

bends of the roadway. As the roadway leisurely goes up round the craggy peak of Mont Durand your footpath continues in the same direction round hairpin bends to the plateau of Tsè des Violettes and from there continues on the level to the **Cabane de Chanrion**.

For the return you should take the eastern bank: go from the hut along the path northwards diagonally across the meadows, cross over a track which leads to the water container and come to the cleft of the Brenay glacier run-off. At the bridge go over the narrow gorge and continue on the far side across the steep flank to the **Col de Tsofeiret**. The plateau of the same name is situated beyond with the delightful marshy lakes. Continue leisurely downhill across the meadows, as if on a terrace, in the direction of the dam. At Giétro alp you meet a roadway again along which you walk the last bit to the top of the dam and then across the dam back to **Mauvoisin**.

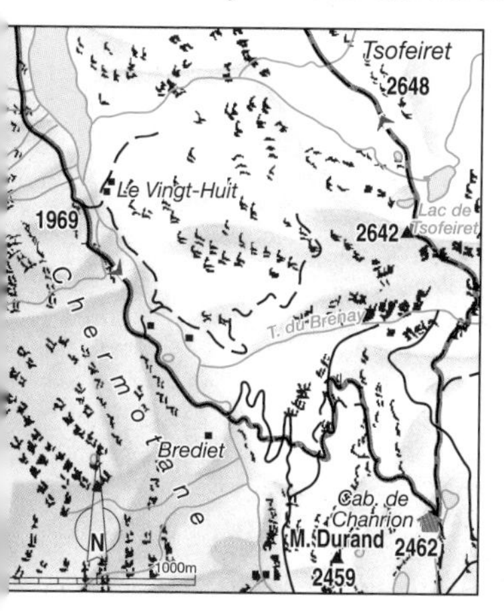

# 38 Combe de l'A

Isolated valley rich in game

## Vichères – La Tsissette – Combe de l'A (Vouasse alp)

**Location:** Liddes, 1346m; beautiful village on the road to the Grand St. Bernard. Bus service to Orsières (MO railway from Martigny) with up to 7 buses a day.
**Starting point:** valley lift station (about 1595m) above Vichières, a small hamlet above the confluence of the Combe de l'A with Val d'Entremont at Liddes, accessible along a partly narrow road, large car park.
**Walking times:** station – La Tsissette 2½ hrs., onward path to the Vouasse alp 1½ hrs., descent 2½ hrs.; total time 6 – 7 hrs.
**Difference in height:** 800m.
**Grade:** long valley walk, on a broad track at the bottom and a good narrow path above. No facilities on the way.
**Worth seeing:** the Combe de l'A is not only one of the quietest high valleys in the Valais, but is also one of the areas with the highest game population – together with hares, marmots, chamoix and deer you can see stags and ibex, and quite often eagles flying above.

Because of the length of the walk it's recommended that you drive up to the car park at the valley station of the small Vichières lift area to save yourself about 480m in altitude on the ascent from Liddes.
At the bend in the road below the valley lift station the track branches off into the **Combe de l'A**. Almost without gaining any height at first it crosses into therift valley of the Torrent de la Chaux and then ascending, leads on the ot-

*The small Vouasse alpine hut in the top Combe de l'A.*

her side round a mountain ridge to the bottom of the **Torrent de l'A** valley. You could take a shortcut across part of the track along a steep footpath, but it's much more pleasant on the track which continues towards the edge at **'Le Creux'** (1721m) where there's a junction with the direct ascent from Liddes. Here the track curves back into the Combe, and after one kilometre the wood recedes and there's an open view into the bottom of the valley and of the steep flanks on both sides. Only a short way below **Tsissette alp** (2005 m) cross the stream on a bridge and climb up to the old huts. As you take a well-earned rest you will have the best chance here of watching the marmots as they dart about.

It's well worth continuing along a good path below the rocky flanks of the wild Les Echessettes summit to the high mountain pasture at **Vouasse** (2393m) where there is a bubbling mountain stream below and cushions of the most beautiful flowers on the right and left of the path.

If you are still not totally worn out and want to bag the view over the other side into Val Ferret, climb up the grassy slopes easily along some tracks westwards to the notch at 2679m and to the 'Basset', 2765m, located a bit further up and with better views.

The descent is back down the ascent path.

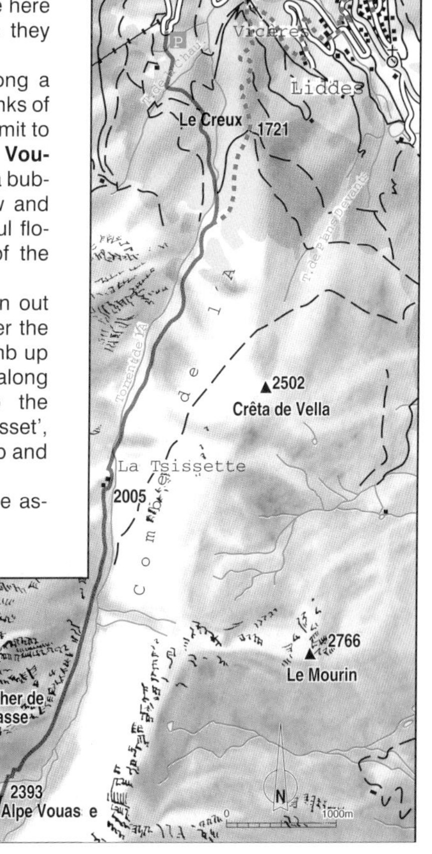

# 39 Cabane du Vélan, 2569 m

Marvellous vantage point on the south side of the Grand Combin

## Bourg St. Pierre – Cabane du Vélan

**Location:** Bourg St. Pierre, 1632m; highest village in Val d'Entremont. Bus service to Orsières (up to 7 buses a day, 25 mins. journey; two buses come directly from Martigny, or else from there by Bernard-Express to Orsières).
**Starting point:** Bourg St. Pierre; if you are travelling by car, you can in theory drive up almost another 150m in altitude along the alpine path, but there is only a small amount of parking space – so it's better to start from the village.
**Walking times:** ascent to the Vélan hut 3 – 3½ hrs.; return about 2½ hrs.; total time 5½ – 6 hrs.
**Difference in height:** 940m.
**Grade:** good mountain paths with adequate waymarkers.
**Food and accommodation:** the Cabane du Vélan was destroyed by fire at the beginning of the 90s; it has been restored by the SAC, in particular the Genf branch. In the summer season the hut warden is present and offers drinks and plain food. We can recommend an overnight stay and the hut is rarely overcrowded in the summer (Tel: 027/7871313).
**Worth seeing:** the eastern centre of Bourg St. Pierre; view from the hut on the south side of the Grand Combin.

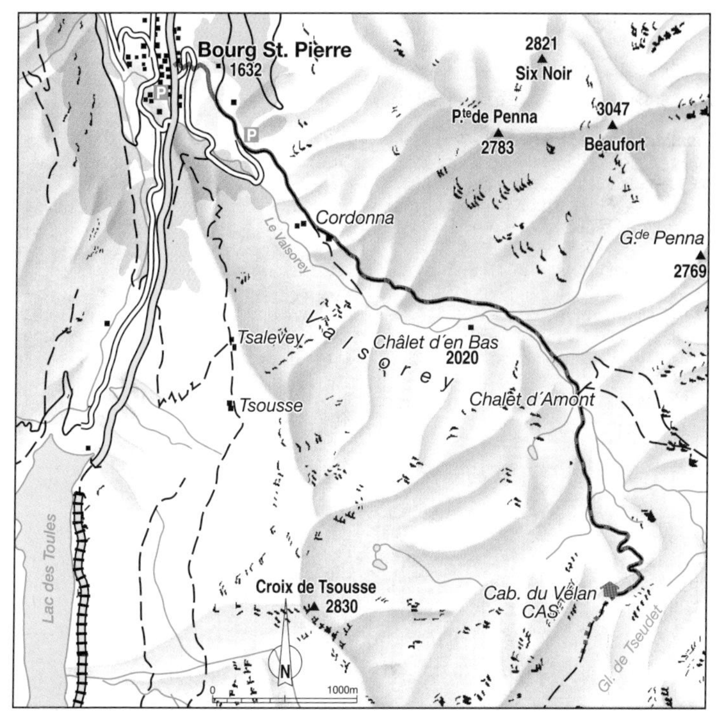


From **Bourg St. Pierre** go along the roadway below the main road and up the Valsorey valley; you can take a shortcut across the wide sweep of a bend into the bottom of the valley along a footpath. Now continue up the valley, only going slightly uphill past the Cordonna huts and, keeping on the sunny slope, you come to a small gorge. Passing above it you soon reach the alluvial plain at the confluence of the streams from the Valsorey and Tseudet glaciers; here the steep hut ascent branches off left to the Cabane de Valsorey at the Grand Combin. Your path leads on the right into a valley basin formed from the side moraine of the Tseudet glacier and winds round to the morainal ridge; a wild view opens up here down onto the glacial tongue. In a few minutes you have reached the **Cabane du Vélan**.
The descent goes back the same way.

*Left: Mont Vélan forms the high alpine background near Liddes.*

# 40 Col du Bastillon, 2757m

Grand viewing balcony between Mont Blanc and Grand Combin

## La Pierre alp – Combe de Drône – Col du Bastillon

**Location:** Bourg St. Pierre, 1632m.
**Starting point:** turn-off from the little road to La Pierre alp, 2093m, about 500m above the skiing area of Super St. Bernard. Parking at the sides of this short stretch of path to the alp.
**Walking times:** ascent 2½ hrs., descent 1¾ hrs.; total time 4¼ hrs.
**Difference in height:** 670m.
**Grade:** easy walk. The path gets lost in the middle section on a meadow, but becomes obvious again from the large rock onwards (joining of the path from Grand St. Bernard, Walk 41). No facilities on the way.
**Worth seeing:** view back of the Grand Combin and when you reach the pass, the overwhelming view of Mont Blanc and its lesser peaks and down to the three lakes, the Lacs de Fenêtre.
There's also a lake above the Combe de Drône, the Grand Le.

Half a day is enough for the walk which takes a good four hours – so in summer you can still start out in the afternoon at 2pm if you intend stopping overnight at the Grand St. Bernard hospice (recommended both because of its special atmosphere and inexpensively good accommodation as well as the St. Bernard dog breeding farm).
The walk goes from **La Pierre alp** along a good, marked path at first beside the stream to the point 2187m, where it crosses over and leads into the middle ground of the **Combe de Drône**. The path gets lost on the slightly inclined grassy surface (about 2300m), but the direction is quite clearly indicated. The waymarked route from the Col des Chevaux (above to the south) is reached at a large rock. A little later cross the stream again and on wide hairpin bends to the north-west proceed to a gently inclined area and the path leads across towards the **Col du Bastillon** which you could see from a long way off. Lakes like eyes to the left and the right.
Zigzag steeply up the last few metres over scree to the col from where there's a sudden and spectacular panorama: Grand Golliat, Mont Blanc, Gran-

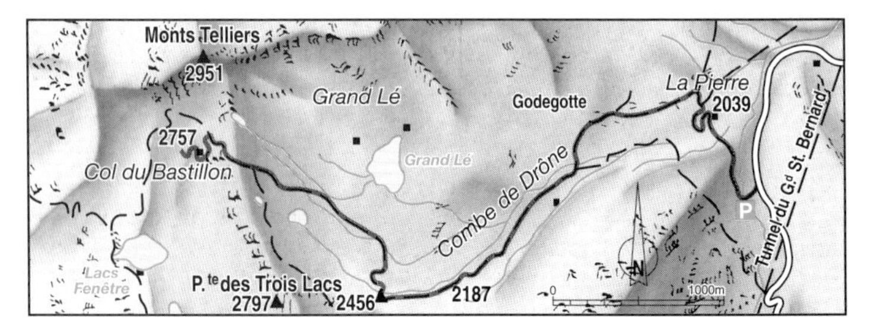

*View from the Col du Bastillon of Mont Blanc and Grandes Jorasses.*

des Jorasses, Mont Dolent and behind you, the Grand Combin with its two peaks, and Mont Vélan nearby. The Swiss part of Val Ferret is a long way down, and the three Lacs de Fenêtre are directly below the steep sloping rocks. A military hut lies to the east below the col.
Descend back down the same way.

# 41 Three cols of the Grand St. Bernard

Round walk with three heights between Combin and Mont Blanc

## Col du Grand St. Bernard – Col des Chevaux – Col du Bastillon – Fenêtre de Ferret – Col du Grand St. Bernard

**Location:** Martigny, 476m, in the Rhône valley.
**Starting point:** Col du Grand St. Bernard, 2469m. You reach the famous pass which crosses the Swiss / Italian border, up the Val d'Entremont from Martigny. Do not forget your passport or identity card since you enter Italian territory at the end of the walk. There's a regular bus service to the Grand St. Bernard. If you are travelling by car, you can park at the hospice.
**Walking times:** Grand St. Bernard – Col des Chevaux 1½ hrs., Col des Chevaux – Col du Bastillon 1½ hrs., Col de Bastillon – Fenêtre de Ferret 1½ hrs., Fenêtre de Ferret – Grand St. Bernard 1 hr.; total time 5½ – 6 hrs.
**Difference in height:** 950m.
**Highest point:** Col du Bastillon, 2757m.
**Grade:** high alpine walk on well-made, marked paths which often go across steep precipices. Lack of vertigo and sure-footedness essential.
**Food and accommodation:** only in the hospice at the Grand St. Bernard.
**Worth seeing:** superb views from the Col du Bastillon down the mountain side and into the distance; world famous St. Bernard dog breeding farm of the Benedictine monks on the pass.

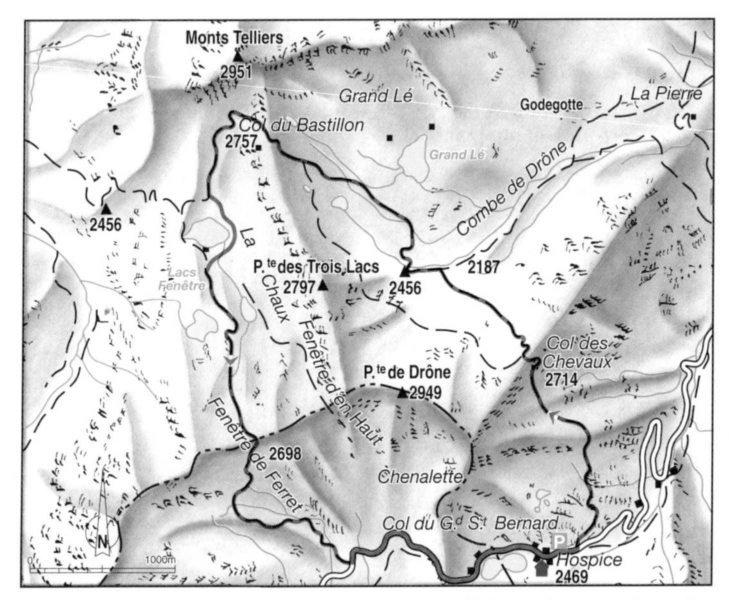


From the **Grand St. Bernard** hospice go on the Swiss side 100m down the road and left steeply up the rocks along a good path laid by the military. Without any great variation in height continue across rocky ground interspersed with grass to the **Col des Chevaux**, 2714m; the huge Grand Combin is in the east. Now follows a steep, but not dangerous descent on a good path into the Combe de Drôme. You reach Walk 40 at the large rock. Cross the stream and wind up round wide hairpin bends onto a stony, gently inclined area where the path runs across towards the col. You finally go steeply up over scree onto the **Col du Bastillon**, from where there's a stunning view of the Mont Blanc peaks. Descend steeply below vertical rocks into a cirque of scree and further down to the three Lacs de Fenêtre, 2456m. Go at the east side around the lower lake and between the other two lakes to the south, towards the already visible **Fenêtre de Ferret**, 2698m. (unusual rock strata on either side). At the Fenêtre you reach the Swiss / Italian border. Descend on a less good path to the road over the pass that you could see from the Fenêtre and go back along this to the **Grand St. Bernard** hospice, passing two border stations on the way.

*Left: view from the Col de Bastillion of the Golliat peaks and the Lacs de Fenêtre.*

# 42 Tête de Ferret, 2713m

Mountain on the border between the Italian and Swiss Val Ferret

## Ferret – La Gouille – Combe des Fonds – Tête de Ferret

**Location:** La Fouly, 1593m; bus service to Orsières (up to 7 buses a day, 25 minute journey); Orsières can easily be reached on the Bernard-Express from Martigny station.
**Starting point:** Ferret, 1700m; highest village in Val Ferret, the road is only open to general traffic for another 1km past the village. Stopping place on the Tour du Mont Blanc (TMB). Buses via Fouly to Martigny. From the Fouly – Ferret road a track bears right shortly after the houses of Les Granges down to the Ferret stream; you are not allowed to drive beyond the bridge, so park here.
**Walking times:** Ferret – La Gouille 1¾ hrs., ascent to the Tête de Ferret 2 hrs., descent to the Petit Col Ferret ¼ hr., return to Ferret 2 hrs.; total time 6 hrs.
**Difference in height:** 1020m.
**Grade:** easy mountain walk on good paths, but steep on the summit section; alternative across the grassy north ridge without paths, but on open ground.
**Food and accommodation:** restaurant in Ferret (a base with accommodation on the TMB). No facilities on the way.
**Worth seeing:** Val Ferret is one of the quiet Valaisan valleys surrounded by high mountains.
The wild eastern precipices of the Mont Blanc group with Mont Dolent, Tour Noir and the peaks around Saleina and Orny glaciers are on one side, steep wood-covered flanks below in the east, vineyards above, and yet further up the valley desolate rock faces up to the summits. From the Col and Tête de Ferret there's also a view into the Italian part of Val Ferret, and from the Tête you can see across to the Grand Combin.

*Tête de Ferret summit: the Combin towers up in the east above the horizon.*

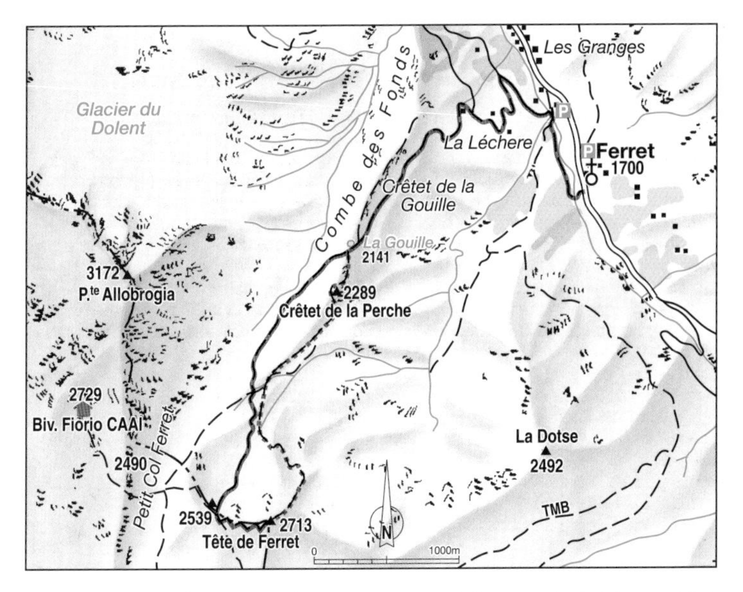


From **Ferret** go along the path at the upper end down to the bridge and follow the stream down the valley until the point after about 500m where the meadow track joins (starting point for car users). Now go along this for about another half kilometre gently uphill until a path bears left before the wood. This soon turns into an earthy path and ascends across an area of pasture-land until you meet the track just before La Léchere alp. From here there's a well-marked path uphill along the Crêtet de la Gouille to a cleft in the ridge where there's a small lake which is occasionally dried up (**La Gouille**, 2141m). The path now runs on the right into the upper **Combe des Fonds** and goes along behind the Crêtet de la Perche across the little area of sparse meadows below **Tête de Ferret** and then onto the col situated to the west of it (Petit Col Ferret is behind the rock rising to the west). From here you zigzag steeply up to Tête de Ferret.
An alternative which is more demanding, but scenically more beautiful, is the direct ascent from the little lake of La Gouille over the grassy Crêtet de la Perche to the plateau. From here it curves round widely to the left, without losing height, to the grass-covered north ridge of the Tête; ascend steeply with no paths, and yet easily, along the uppermost ridge with beautiful views to the top.
Go down the ascent path via the Petit Col Ferret.

# 43 Bisse du Trient – Col de Balme, 2204m

From the Trient glacier to the 'box seat' in front of Mont Blanc

## Col de la Forclaz – Trient glacier – Col de Balme – Trient

**Location:** Martigny, 476m; central point and traffic junction at the sharp bend of the Rhône in western Valais. Station on the SBB line Lausanne – Sion. Trient, 1279m; small village on the road to Chamonix. Post bus service from Martigny over the Col de la Forclaz (about 4 buses a day, 40 minute journey, 35km from Martigny).
**Starting point:** Col de la Forclaz, 1526m; pass on the stretch of road between Martigny and Chamonix. Post bus (5 minute journey from Trient).
**Walking times:** La Forclaz – Chalet du Glacier (Trient glacier) 50 mins., ascent to Les Grands 1¾ hrs., mountain path to Col de Balme 1¼ hrs., descent to Trient 1¾ hrs. (return to the pass by bus, or else it's an hour longer); a good 5½ or 6½ hrs in total.
**Difference in height:** 680m.
**Grade:** good mountain paths with adequate waymarkers (part of the Tour du Mont Blanc (TMB).
**Food and accommodation:** Hotel-Restaurant at the Col de la Forclaz. Chalet du Glacier – the restaurant is open below the Trient glacier in the summer season (refreshments, plain food). Refuge Les Grands, 2113m, situated in the side valley of the Grand glacier on a meadow; private hut belonging to a branch of the Geneva SAC, mostly open in summer (drinks), but you shouldn't rely on this since it can also be closed for a few days. Restaurant on the Col de Balme, 2204m.
**Worth seeing:** the glacial fields of the Trient plateau, the most northern peak of the Mont-Blanc group; there are beautiful views from the area around the Les Grands hut especially, and also down into the Trient valley. The Col de Balme finally allows you open views into the Chamonix valley with Mont Blanc towering above everything.

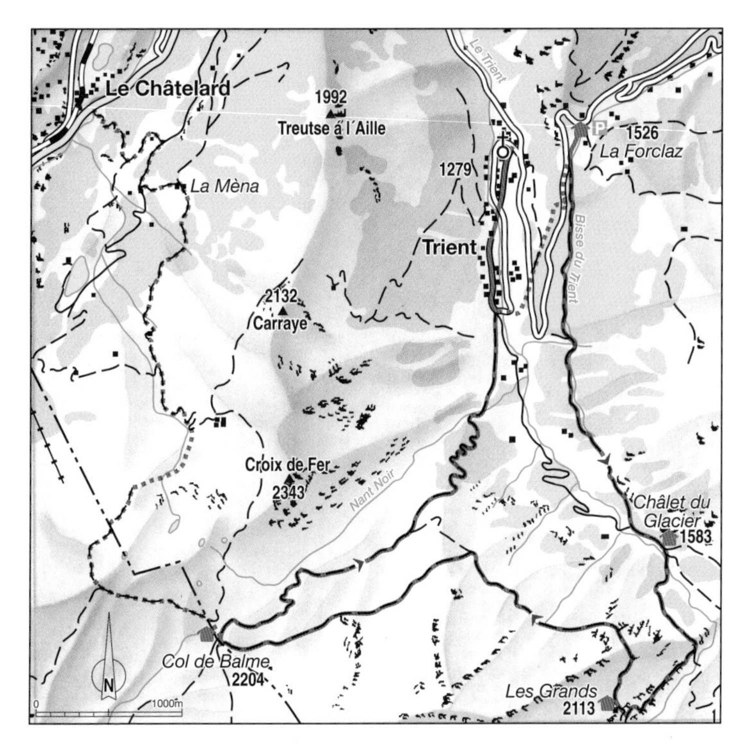


At the **Col de la Forclaz** follow the signpost to the water channel and up the valley with very little variation in height. In between times there are views down into the valley and you reach the Chalet du Glacier in the valley bottom without any great effort and meanwhile a good kilometre away from the tongue of the **Trient glacier**. Cross the stream and go uphill through a thin wood to reach the corner above the confluence of the Grand valley at some beautiful crags. The path winds up a strangely sloping terrace of meadows between two areas of rock, then via a flight of constructed steps through the upper rocks to the mountain pasture lying above with the Les Grands hut. Have a good rest here, especially if the hut warden is present who can provide you with drinks.

*Left: Les Grands hut at the glacier of the same name.*

But there's still another increase: after several minutes across terrain covered in a few picturesque Swiss pines you come to an edge where the view opens out northwards and back down into the Trient valley. You now proceed along a panoramic path, but with some ups and downs, until you find yourself standing on the **Col de Balme** above the Chamonix valley opposite Mont Blanc.

*Looking from the Col de Balme across the Chamonix valley to Mont Blanc.*

*The Trient glacier flows behind Les Grands below the Pointe d'Orny into the valley.*

If you do not have to return to the Col de la Forclaz for the car, using a good map, descend on the west side of the pass round the Croix de Fer a highly recommended detour – for which you should allow another 2 hrs – to the MC railway station at Châtelard and return by train to Martigny – this is by far the most beautiful way round the mountain. Otherwise descend directly on the path to **Trient**, across the meadow slopes above the Nant Noir stream, then down some steep zigzags to the bottom of the valley. Either return the 1,5km to the village (bus stop) or climb up in about 1 hr. to the water channel on the Col de la Forclaz.

# 44 Gorges du Trient – Les Marécottes

Bold view down the deep gorge and a unique railway experience

## Vernayaz – Pont de Gueuroz – La Tailla – Les Marécottes

**Location and Starting point:** Vernayaz, 452m; situated about 5km before Martigny and well-known as being the start of the Gorges du Trient; station for the SBB and MC lines and the rail link from Martigny to Châtelard / Chamonix, which you use for the return.

**Destination:** Les Marécottes, 1100m; situated with Le Trétien, Salvan and Les Granges high above the Trient on a terrace with beautiful views, good train connections with Martigny and Chamonix, a train almost every hour in summer.

**Walking times:** Vernayaz – Pont de Gueuroz ¾ hrs., via La Tailla to the Trient stream ¾ hrs., ascent to Les Marécottes 1 hr.; total time 2½ hrs.

**Difference in height:** 580m.

**Highest point:** at Les Marécottes station, 1030m.

**Grade:** good hiking paths.

**Food and accommodation:** restaurant at the Pont de Gueuroz, otherwise in Vernayaz and Marécottes.

**Worth seeing:** great views into the Rhône valley at the start, then from the bridge an amazing view down the deep gorge (200m to the water) – be sure not to let anything drop because there's a path along the bottom of the gorge. We recommended that you visit the Alpine zoo in Les Marécottes before returning into the Rhône valley on the rack-railway along a truly audacious track, which is another highlight of this walk. It's also pleasant to walk down into the gorge as well.

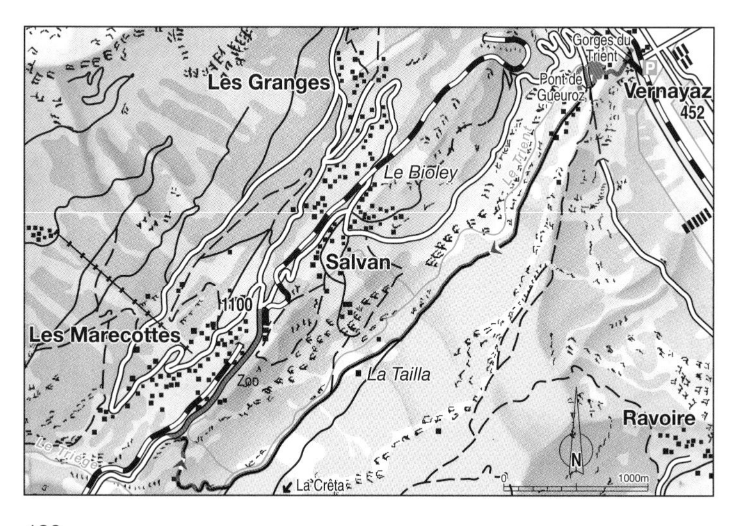

*Salvan-Marécottes lies above the Trient gorge, dominated by the Luisin.*

The rather steep path onto the band of rock starts immediately next to the MC station and at the entrance to the Trient gorge in **Vernayaz**. On its upper section you can take a few paces over to the edge of a precipice looking almost vertically down into the Rhône valley. Shortly after that you come to the road with the restaurant and the **'Pont de Gueuroz'** bridge – built in the thirties, it has since become rather decrepit and is presently being replaced with a new bridge.
Your route now follows the track up the valley on the south side of the Gorges du Trient, then branches off right at **La Tailla** from the main path leading to La Crêta and goes to the stream. It follows this for another kilometre up the valley to another turn-off where, again to the right, it leads to the bridge over the Trient. The path goes uphill again on the other side and halfway to the village, gives you a view into the Trétien gorge. Soon after that you come to the road between Les Marécottes and Trétien. Not far along this you reach the holiday resort; you also go past the Alpine zoo – if time allows you shouldn't miss the chance to visit it.
The return by rack-railway into the Rhône valley is the culmination of the walk: the train rattles along an audaciously-laid track back to Vernayaz.

# 45 Mont de l'Arpille, 2085m

Supreme belvedere for Mont Blanc in lovely walking country

## Ravoire – L'Arpille alp– Mont de l'Arpille – Col de la Forclaz

**Location:** Martigny, 47m; interesting small town with some remarkable cultural things to offer and lots of historical buildings. SBB station, junction for the railway link to Châtelard – Chamonix (MC) and of the Bernard-Express (MO).
**Starting point:** Ravoire, 1175m; settlement spread out above the road to the Col de la Forclaz with a beautiful view across western Valais. PTT buses to Martigny (about 5 a day, 30 minute journey, 14km). Tip: you can drive a little further by car up along a track from Ravoire although this will make the crossing to the Col de la Forclaz more complicated.
**Destination:** Col de la Forclaz, 1526m; pass on the road Martigny – Trient – Chamonix, PTT stop (about 4 buses a day, 35 minutes journey, 20km).
**Walking times:** Ravoire – L'Arpille alp 1¾ hrs., summit climb ¾ hrs., descent to the Col de la Forclaz 1¼ hrs.; total time 3½ – 4 hrs.
**Difference in height:** 910m.
**Grade:** easy mountain walk on good, marked paths.
**Food and accommodation:** guest houses in Ravoire and on the Col de la Forclaz. No food on the way.
**Worth seeing:** beautiful high alpine meadows, wonderful display of flowers in early summer. Wide panorama of Mont Blanc, Dents du Midi, Morcles-Gruppe, Rhône valley and Grand Combin.

*View from Mont de l'Arpille of Salvan-Marecottes with Dent de Morcles above the Rhône valley.*

From the bus terminus in **Ravoire** go uphill along the hiking path diagonally south-westwards, alternately across open ground and through short stretches of wood, past some solitary houses and a small settlement (Chez Pillet). In the 'Grande Communaux' wood, a little above the clearing of 'Les Clous', you meet the track mentioned at the starting point in the introduction.
Continue along this for only a short way and then it narrows to a forest track and leads steeply up to **L'Arpille**. The waymarking is a bit confusing at the huts: you are sign-posted left to an old path which soon gets rather lost, but then also leads up to the summit.

The better path, however, starts a little way above a water container up from the hut and passes the pre-summit covered in crosses (2051m) to reach the extensive flat summit of **Mont de l'Arpille** with windswept trees and avalanche protection barriers. If the weather's good you could easily while away the whole day up here.
On the descent follow the path at the western edge of the alpine plateau of 'Plan du Gy', at the end of which you enter a wood and finally zigzag downhill to the **Col de la Forclaz**. Return by bus to Martigny.

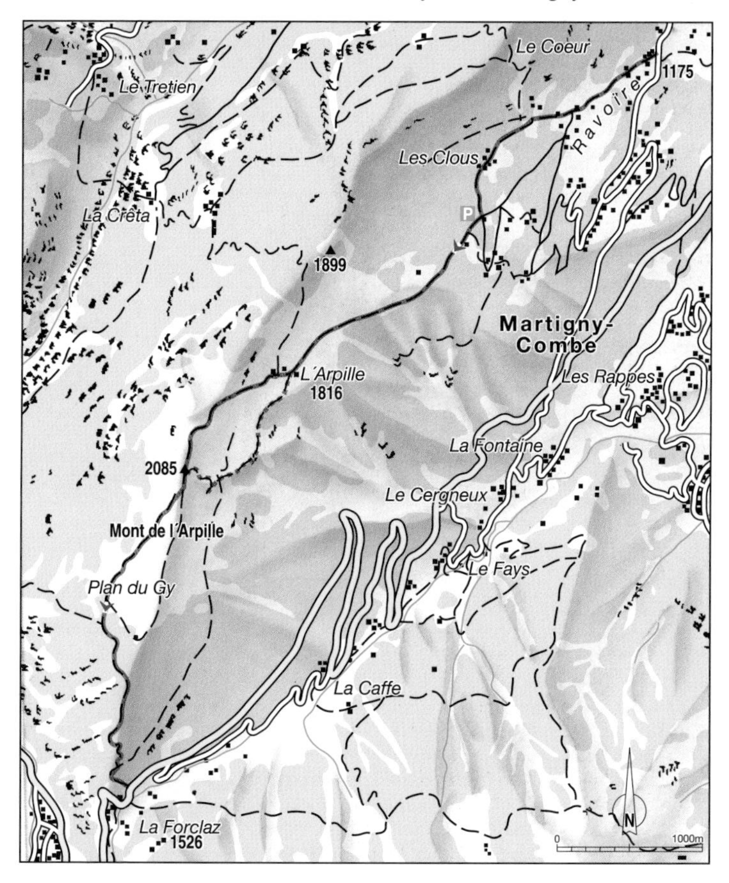

# 46 Lac d'Emosson – Col de Barberine, 2481m

Expansive view of the Mont Blanc massif

**Lac d'Emosson – Barberine alp – Col de Barberine**

**Location:** Finhaut, 1298m.
**Starting point:** Lac d'Emosson dam, 1960m. Cable railway (two sections, connected by a mountain tramway) from Le Châtelard (MC-railway). Also accessible along a tarmac road from Finhaut. Five hairpin bends take you down the 650 vertical metres. From the car park there's a short descent to the entrance of the tunnel, 1930m. Parking also possible next to the tunnel entrance.
**Walking times:** Lac d'Emosson – Barberine alp 1½ hrs., Barberine alp – Col de Barberine 1½ hrs.; descent 2 hrs.; total time 5 hrs.
**Difference in height:** 550m.
**Grade:** easy walk, sure-footedness essential in the upper part.
**Food and accommodation:** only in the restaurant at the dam.
**Worth seeing:** brilliant view from the dam of the Lac d'Emosson of Mont Blanc. You can walk across the wall and climb up along a small road on the other side to the 180m higher Lac du Vieux Emosson, 2205m. Footprints and remains of dinosaurs have been found in this area. A small museum with the figure of a dinosaur in front above the dam and restaurant.

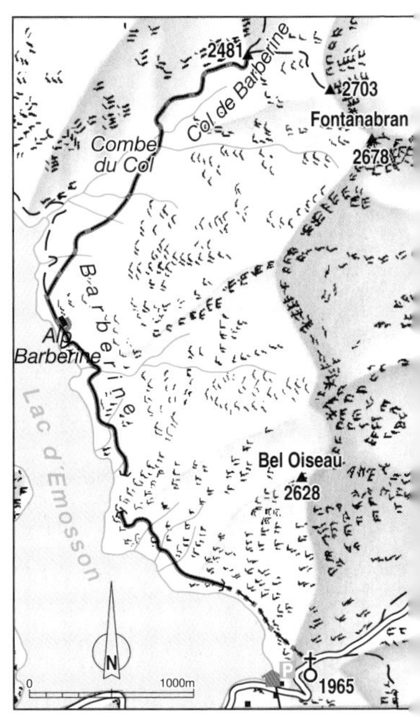


Go about 850 to 900 paces, fairly on the level, through the lit tunnel at **Lac d'Emosson** to the other side of the ridge. Another short tunnel follows before the little tarmac road leads up and down across interesting terrain above the lake to the **Barberine alp**. As you take a rest and then descend a short way onto a ridge there's a marvellous view of the highest mountain of the Alps and its lesser peaks.
Just behind the hut a board points to the right to the Col de Barberine. The path leads steeply uphill at first and then continues fairly on the level into the small high valley of the Combe du Col. After crossing the stream it goes up more steeply across sloping meadows towards a rocky gorge which you cross over along tracks in the scree. The mountain path winds up above across eroded slate slopes, to the **Col de Barberine** where the distant view

is obscured of the surrounding peaks which are partly reflected in the lake. If you still feel fit enough then we can recommend the short walk to the Fontanabran, 2702m, which rises above the col to the south-east. In doing so, all your expectations will be reallised.
The descent goes back down the ascent path.

*The Lac d'Emosson runs fjord-like towards the striated Mont Ruan.*

# 47 Lac de Salanfe, 1942m

At the foot of the wild Dents du Midi

## Salvan – Valon de Van – Lac de Salanfe

**Location and starting point:** Salvan, 934m; situated on the interesting stretch of railway between Martigny – Chatelard – Chamonix on a sunny terrace above the Trient gorge.
**Walking times:** Salvan – Van d'en Haut 1½ hrs., onward path to the Salanfe reservoir 1½ hrs., return to Salvan 2 hrs.; total time 5 hrs.
**Difference in height:** 1010m.
**Highest point:** restaurant at the Salanfe lake, 1942m.
**Grade:** good hiking paths, part of the Tour de Val de Trient.
**Food and accommodation:** restaurant at the reservoir, open in the high season.
**Worth seeing:** the Vallon de Van is a dramatically fissured side valley, which drains the large basin of Salanfe below the Dents du Midi and Tour Salliére down to the lower Rhône valley. The delightful large deep-blue reservoir lies below the sloping meadows of the Salanfe Alps and in contrast, the rocks and glaciers on the Dents du Midi rise above and the north-eastern flank of the Tour Salière seems quite inhospitable with its darks rocks into which a small glacier lies embedded.

If you're in a hurry you can drive by car or taxi along the very narrow road into the Vallon de Van thereby shortening the walk by about half – but there still remains a general unspoilt impression on this 'stretch'.

*The Tour Sallière is mirrored in the water of Lac de Salanfe.*

From the station follow the path signed with TVT (Tour du Val de Trient) to Les Granges (a shortcut from the road). The path continues through the meadows above the village to the wood where you soon meet the road. Stay on this for just under 300m, then the footpath bears left and goes across a rocky flank around an edge of ground into the **Vallon de Van**. At a junction at the houses of Van d'en Haut you come to the road again which ends here.

It now goes uphill as a footpath and a rough forest track until the terrain eventually opens out again and you come to the really small dam – you would not imagine that such a large reservoir could be found here! Then it's only another few paces to the top of the dam and an open view into this enormous basin. Keeping to the right you quickly come to the small hut where you also can get drinks and snacks in summer.

If you want to climb up higher it takes less than an hour to reach the **Col du Jorat** situated to the north (2210m), which not only gives you a view of Lake Geneva but also Salanfe lake and down into the Rhône valley.

The return is back down the ascent path.

# 48 Croix de Javerne – Cabane Tourche – Rionda

At the foot of the Dent de Morcles with a view out to Lake Geneva.

**Morcles – La Forcle – Croix de Javerne – Cabane Tourche – Rionda alp – L'Au de Morcles – Morcles**

**Location:** Lavey les Bains, 417m; small settlement with thermal baths at St. Maurice at the narrow part in the lower Rhône valley; railway station.
**Starting point:** Morcles, 1160m; tiny, remote village on a small terrace on the steep slope of the Morcles massif above the Rhône valley, a steep and narrow road goes uphill with no less than 29 bends. Post bus service to St. Maurice (6 buses a day, just under 30 minute journey, 10km). Parking in Morcles or on the road continuing above La Forcle, 1395m.
**Walking times:** Morcles – La Forcle ¾ hrs., ascent to Croix de Javerne 2½ hrs., mountain path to Cabane Tourche ½ hr., onward path to Rionda alp ½ hr., descent to La Forcle 1 hr., back to Morcles 20 mins.; total time 5 – 6 hrs. (4½ hrs., if you choose La Forcle as the starting point).
**Difference in height:** 1040m.
**Highest point:** Cabane Tourche, 2198m.
**Grade:** not a difficult walk on good paths, also partly on meadow roads.
**Food and accommodation:** Cabane Tourche, in the high season there's a custodian who prepares simple meals, but in June and September only at the weekends (make enquiries in Morcles); possible overnight accommodation, always open.
**Worth seeing:** the drive to Morcles and its location are worth the trip in themselves, but the higher you climb, the more impressive the view – the Rhône valley, Lake Geneva, the Dents du Midi opposite and the Mont Blanc massif or the interesting striated layering of the rocks on the Dents de Morcles.
The description here is of an exceedingly strenuous mountain walk, but which is compensated by memorable impressions. If you are in your own car you can save just under 250 vertical metres by driving up beyond La Forcle, which will shorten the walking time by one hour.

From **Morcles** go along the path across the sloping meadows above the village and below L'Aiguille rocky ridge; you come to the road again near to La Forcle. You should leave your car at the latest at the turn-off of the alpine road into the Morcles basin since this is where you will end the walk on the

*After a sudden fall in temperature the new snow shows up the striations on the Dent de Morcles with unusual clarity.*

descent. Partly on the road, partly across the meadows between the bends continue uphill across La Rosseline alp and past the ski hut at Le Martenau until on the following steep slope the track makes its way round several bends into the area of the forest boundary. Above the alpine hut of Le Crêtelet a footpath branches off on the last bend of the track and along this you climb up the final slope to the ridge and there's now an open view to the east. In a few minutes you reach the furthermost point at the **Croix de Javerne**, and also the first magnificent viewpoint. The path back along the broad ridge and on to **Cabane Tourche** is an entertaining stroll 'on top of the world'.
After a well-earned break in this beautiful hut you continue across to **Rionda** which you can see opposite, along many pages from the book of 'millions of years of geology' on the steep slope below the Dents de Morcles crags. The descent is now very steep, but only down the first 350 vertical metres, when you switch to a meadow road again (or take a shortcut down another steep 150 vertical metres) which leads into the basin-shaped valley below **L'Au de Morcles** and crosses it on a gentle downhill slope. In the end go directly along below the rock face of Le Martenau to Le Forcle and back to **Morcles**.

# 49 Pointe de Bellevue, 2042m

Beautiful isolated walk near Lake Geneva

**Portes de Culet – Pointe de Bellevue – Combe de Dreveneuse – Prè Fleuri – Chalet Neuf – Portes de Culet**

**Location and starting point:** Morgins, 1333m; holiday resort just before the French border (Pas de Morgins), and Muraz, 402m; small village a few kilometres north of Monthey. Both have a good bus service with Monthey; but the starting point at Portes de Culet, 1787m, can only be reached by car or taxi. Parking at the top of the pass.
**Walking times:** Portes de Culet – Pointe de Bellevue ¾ hrs., descent into the Combe de Dreveneuse ½ hr., return via Prè Fleuri to the Chalet Neuf 1 hr., ascent to the pass 20 mins.; total time about 2½ hrs.
**Difference in height:** 450m.
**Grade:** easy mountain walk up to the summit, then on narrow paths into the Combe and round over the Prè Fleuri ridge.
**Food and accommodation:** in the Chalet Neuf, 1692m; privately owned, situated on the roadway from Muraz just below the top of the pass at the end of the round walk.
**Worth seeing:** wonderful view from the summit of the Dents du Midi, across the Rhône valley of the western Bernese Alps and as far as Lake Geneva. The Combe de Dreveneuse encircled by loose rocky slopes is an oasis of tranquillity; the small self-catering hut there belongs to the community of Muraz, where you can enquire about the key; it is a really inviting place for a longish rest.

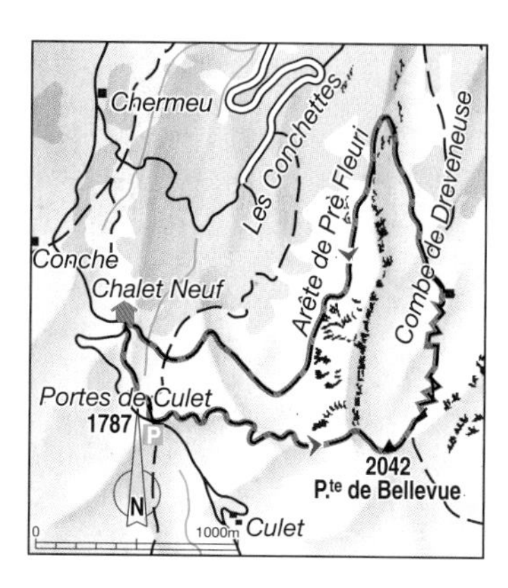


From the col of **Portes de Culet** (signpost) follow the path to the east up across the grassy ridge, but after only 100 vertical metres it becomes considerably flatter. Climb up along the edge of precipices to the point where the Prè-Fleuri ridge joins and come along an almost level path to the **Pointe de Bellevue** where there's a marvellous panorama, as the name suggests.
A steep little path leads a few paces down on the eastern side of the summit across a gravel slope to the north into the **Combe de Dreveneuse**. Then it goes through a thin stand of trees in the valley and across meadows to the nearby Refuge de Dreveneuse (Chalet Neuf).
Do not continue descending in the bottom of the valley (you could descend 1500m from here down to Muraz), but go immediately left along the path across the slope and then make a short ascent onto the **Prè Fleuri** ridge.

*View from Pointe de Bellevue to France across the Conche col; Mont de Grange on the left.*

The path follows the ridge uphill for a short way and then on the other side high above the valley floor, it crosses the scree slopes into the valley beyond. It leads eventually to the **Chalet Neuf** almost on the level around another ridge.
From here take the direct path to Portes de Culet nearby, or if you prefer a more level route, you can also follow the roadway.

# 50 Lac de Tanay

Small jewel of a lake at the north-western tip of the Valais

## Miex – Lac de Tanay – Miex

**Location:** Vouvry, 380 – 440m; situated on the Rhône a few kilometres before it flows into Lake Geneva. Railway station for the link between St. Gingolph (Lake Geneva) – Monthey; trains and buses.
**Starting point:** Miex, 900 – 1050m; small settlement high above the Rhône valley with several areas. Bus service to Vouvry (about 5 buses a day, 20 minute journey time). Parking a few metres past the highest village area (Le Flon) at the start of the steep roadway.
**Walking times:** Miex / Le Flon – Lac de Tanay 1½ hrs., walk round the lake to the Col de Tanay ¾ hrs., return to Miex ¾ hrs.; total time 3 hrs.
**Difference in height:** 390m.
**Highest point:** Col de Tanay, 1440m.
**Grade:** easy walk, although a very steep ascent to the lake.
**Food and accommodation:** restaurants at Lac de Tanay; there are also plenty of places to stay overnight, so that you can take several days and explore the area at your leisure.
**Worth seeing:** it's a total surprise to find this lake lying high above the Rhône valley, not far from Lake Geneva and surrounded by sheer crags. The lake is under environmental protection. It's well worth climbing another 2 hours up from the lake and making an ascent of the northern summit of Le Grammont (good paths) at which point Lake Geneva lies literally at your feet.
**Remarks:** in the area of ascent, an extremely steep small road also goes up to Lac de Tanay, only suitable for four-wheel drives or mini-buses from Miex-Vésenand.

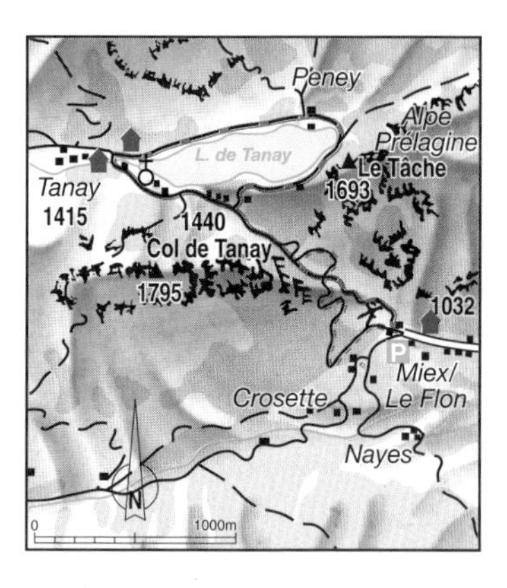


At the upper end of the car park at **Miex / Le Flon** the steep footpath begins to the right and takes a short cut across the first bend of the roadway and meets it again at the second bend. The path zigzags up across the boulder-strewn steep flank, crosses the roadway again, and eventually rejoins it just below the Col de Tanay. The path now goes left, leisurely along the bank of **Lac de Tanay** to the small settlement of Tanay.
After taking some refreshment you should at least walk round the lake. Go along the north bank as far as the eastern tip and then along the south bank back to the Col de Tanay; in so doing you realise that the lake has an inflow (at Tanay), but not an outlet – this occurs under the ground in the fissured limestone.

If you do not wish to descend the steep way you came, after a 100m ascent from the eastern end of the lake, return to **Miex** down a cart track across the Alpe Prelagine with beautiful views of the Rhône valley.

*The Lac de Tany with the rocky peak of La Tâche.*

# Index

The numbers behind the headwords relate to the walk numbers or notes in the chapter 'Locations' (L).